WHAT'S
IN MY
BOOK

Laura Watkins

ASCENDING from

EVERLASTING DESTRUCTION

to ETERNAL LIFE

ISBN 979-8-21800-677-8 (Print)
ISBN 978-1-66785-996-5 (eBook)

First Edition

Cover Design and Layout by BookBaby.com Publishing

Published by BookBaby Publishing
7905 N. Crescent Blvd.
Pennsauken, NJ 08110
www.BookBaby.com

Printed in the United States of America

Foreword

What's in My Book: Ascending From Everlasting Destruction to Eternal Life is a book which deals with ways to find happiness and peace in life, in a variety of areas—family, health, business, friendships, etc. Using the author's own personal journey to finding a more meaningful relationship with God as the backdrop for the premise of this information, the author shows how the reader can use not only her own experiences, but specific verses from the Bible to link happiness and a strong spiritual and religious lifestyle.

The strength in this book is the way the author uses her firsthand experiences to illustrate each point she strives to make with reference to finding everyday events that can be strengthened, improved, and healed with a stronger relationship with God. The author strategically intersperses relevant Bible verses to illustrate these points.

Dedication

First, I dedicate this book to God the Father, the Son, and the Holy Spirit for without Their creation and love, I am nothing.

To the Five-Fold Ministry, apostles, prophets, evangelist, preachers, teachers, old and young, founders and new members, may God continue to guide you in His way of teaching His Holy word.

To the brave men and women of the Armed Forces past and present, who stood on the carpet, raised your right hand, and took the oath to serve, I honor you for "Standing the Watch." May God bless you all. Chief Yeoman (Surface Warfare), United States Navy (Retired).

To the readers of this book, I want to encourage you to allow God to do a new thing for you! Just try asking, believing, and seeking Him. For through the Son of God, and the help of the Holy Spirit all things are possible.

Acknowledgements

I give honor, praise, and exaltation to our God, Yah, the Father, the Great I Am, the Creator of man, specifically for this purpose of sharing His word and being a messenger throughout the world for Him.

To my parents and sister, the late Harry Lee Watkins Sr., Laura Etta Watkins, and Elaine Marie Brown, I love and miss you all so much. Sister, your Bible study homework saved my life. "'Blessed are the dead who die in the Lord from now on.' …" that they may rest from their labors, and their works follow them" (Revelation 14:13 [NKJV]).

To my loving son Robert, your support, sense of humor and uplifting spirit encourages me to fulfill my right-now goals and dreams.

To my brother Harry and sister-in-law Catrena, I deeply appreciate and love each one of you. To Arnett (Smiley), you have been a part of our family since my childhood. Thank you for being a big brother, comforter, and solid rock for the entire family.

Introduction

"Come see and hear!" Yes, I said, "Come see and hear!" For what's in my book will cause judgement from man and God. Now, allow me to introduce myself. I, Laura Elizabeth Watkins of Nashville, Tennessee was born on April 10, 1967. The youngest of three, my late mother, whom I love dearly, made it verbally clear that I was not supposed to be here. From her own words, she told me, "After I gave your daddy a son (second born), I didn't want any more children." My brother and I are thirteen months apart. But do not feel sorrow for me. Created in Heaven, and sent to Earth by God the Creator, I am here today to tell you what's in my book!

I am a graduate of East Nashville High School (EAST HIGH!!!) and Strayer University with a Bachelor of Science in Business Management. After twenty years of honorable service, I retired from the U.S. Navy as a Chief Petty Officer Yeoman, (Surface Warfare). I am proud of the latter. However, my biggest accomplishment is that I am a faithful messenger of God. I give thanks to my parents who raised me in love and faith. But I must truly give high honor to my late sister, mentor, and spiritual elder Elaine, (Bug as daddy nicknamed her), for helping me to transition back to God on a whole new level. Through her spiritual wisdom, understanding, knowledge, and teachings of God's word, I became inspired to finally author this book. Sister, I miss you, and I cannot thank you enough!

It has always been a lifelong goal for me to author a book. The only problem, I did not have anything in my spirit that I felt worth writing about until now. Coming out of the wilderness at the age of fifty-five, the time is now! I am a single mom of one son. I got married, (not to my son's father), when I was fifty-two, on my sister's birthday (October 5th), in the living room of my childhood home. Unfortunately, things did not work out as planned. Not even a good year or so after the wedding, I found myself divorced from the "head pastor" of a storefront church. Now, I know I am not perfect, and there are always two sides to why a marriage does not work, but I am not ashamed to share my life and what thus says the Lord! I'm excited and have something to teach!

So, here's a quick background of what inspired me to start writing. On May 5, 1988, I left my hometown (Nashville, Tennessee), to start my journey as a sailor in the U.S. Navy. That was the day I took my very first airplane ride to Orlando, Florida. After arriving at the boot-camp facility, I said to myself, "What did I just do?" Let me tell you, my time in bootcamp was not easy. There were times when it became difficult for me because I refused to submit to those appointed over me. Instead of humbling myself, and allowing them to instruct me, I required extra incentive. I remember being awakened at 3:00 a.m., having to wear a black skull cap on my head, and marching to the gymnasium. Once there, others and I endured about an hour of repetitive exercises or Intensive Training (IT). Trust me, after a couple of these, I learned my lesson. Through self-control, faith, and prayer, I transitioned from everlasting destruction to becoming an obedient follower and respected shipmate.

After settling down and learning how to follow and lead, eventually, I would have an opportunity to pick a job to start my new career. The Navy Career Counselor offered me three specific jobs which included: a Yeoman, a Legalman, and a Mess Management Specialist, which was a cook. Now, coming from a family where everyone knew how to "burn" (meaning they really knew how to cook/throw down in the kitchen), except for me, I chose Mess Specialist. In my mind, I wanted to learn how to feed the masses, and even had a vision of coming home after I retired and opening a family-owned soul food restaurant. However, when God has a plan already set for you, He will assign you to the position needed to complete His required works for judgement.

After choosing Mess Specialist, I vividly remember still to this day the Navy Counselor saying to me before graduating from boot-camp, "Nope, you're going to be trained as a Yeoman!" Keeping the description of the Yeoman rating (i.e., job or Military Occupational Specialist (MOS)), brief, we perform a plethora of clerical, legal, and personnel security tasks, in addition to maintaining publications on shore and at sea. So, with new orders in hand, they bussed me from Orlando, Florida to Meridian, Mississippi Yeoman "A" School where the Navy taught me its way of writing for review and approval of Commanders, Captains, Admirals, Joint Staff, and even Congress.

Today, what is my purpose for authoring this book? It is God's plan to use me as His messenger and His personal Yeoman, (also called "Captain's Yeoman or Captain's Writer") to inspire you to read His word. The title triggers one's curiosity. Consider this book to be like a treasure map for your spiritual walk with God. As you turn the pages, you'll have an opportunity to discover your hidden treasures deep inside you which make you rich in the Father. The subtitle,

"Ascending from Everlasting Destruction to Eternal Life" is a word of warning and call to action.

I want to challenge each reader to use this book as your Plan of the Day (POD). Read this and get excited about knowing God's word for yourself! Ask Him to pour His wisdom, understanding and knowledge into you with the help of the Holy Ghost. Ask Him why were you created? Ask Him His purpose for you right now. Get excited!

Finally, I author this book because it is a seed I must sow and water for all humanity to know God the Father, Son, and Holy Spirit are real. It is my mission as a messenger, writer, and "Yeoman" for God to inform you that the Son of God is preparing His return. And for the record, Jesus Christ is not returning with hugs, kisses, candy, and flowers. You do not have to believe me, but I encourage you to pick up God's Book and read it for yourself! When you close this book, do not delay. Get a pen and paper and write down the question, "What's In My Book?!"

May the Lord bless the reader and doer of His word. Amen and Hallelujah!

CONTENTS

Chapter 1: Pick Up Your Bible and Dust It Off 1

Chapter 2: What's in My Mirror? 3

Chapter 3: Woman With a Past Put Your Junk on the Front Lawn 7

Chapter 4: Spirit-Mind Connection and Renewal 19

Chapter 5: Fasting and Prayer 23

Chapter 6: Listen With a Spiritual Ear 29

Chapter 7: Let the Lord Lead 33

Chapter 8: Follow the Lord 39

Chapter 9: Abraham's Seed? 45

Chapter 10: God Gives Us a Choice 49

Chapter 11: God's People Have Problems Too 55

Chapter 12: Using My Pain to Heal Someone Else 61

Chapter 13: God Appoints and Anoints Positions in the Church 65

Chapter 14: Activate Your Blessings Through Fear and Faith 71

Chapter 15: Hungry for God! 75

Chapter 16: Look Up! Jesus Is Coming in the Clouds 79

Chapter 17: Is Everyday Life a Prize? 83

Chapter 18: God Wants Eternal Life for You and Me 87

Chapter 19: What's in Your Book? 103

Bibliography 109

Index 111

CHAPTER 1:

Pick Up Your Bible
and Dust It Off

Where is that book? You know the book, the one that has been collecting dust for several years. The book that explains who, what, when, where, why, and how God created you. Still confused? Well, the book I am talking about is the Holy Bible. Did you find it? All right, now, pick it up and dust it off. Why? Because what is in this book will guide you through God's book, and I pray both will help prepare you to have your name written in the Book of Life. Let me explain.

The Bible I still have today is the New King James Version (NKJV) Holy Bible written by Bishop T.D. Jakes titled *Holy Bible: Woman Thou Art Loosed! Edition* (Jakes 1998). I will never forget when I received it from my sister's good friend, Sheilah. She and other family members came to San Diego, California, to visit me before my very first six-month underway sea deployment with the U.S. Navy. While the rest of the family and I were drinking and having fun, I remember Sheilah quietly sitting by herself, reading that Bible. After days of visiting, the family began packing up to leave. I asked Sheilah if I could keep her Bible to take with me on the ship which was deployed to the Middle East. I knew the entire crew would need prayer and strengthening words of encouragement. Thank God she said yes!

Recently, I spoke with Reverend Sheilah after the passing of my sister. I told her I still had the Bible she gave me years ago. I explained how she too blessed and helped alter my life by giving me her Bible, which was used more now than ever—and dust-free, I may add. We discussed how my long months at sea, in dangerous waters, made me go back to the one true source of comfort and safety: God's word. Although I've grown tremendously in God's wisdom, under-standing, and knowledge, there were times throughout my life I was not seeking Him. I filled my eye gates and ear gates with worldly transgressions. But the God-fearing and spirit-filled elders guided me back to the Holy Book, which I began using for my eternal life transition from darkness to light. In fact, my elders coached me to be vigilant of what I was allowing to enter, not only in my body but in my Spirit. I had to switch on my light and turn around my mirror in order to see inside of me. Matthew 6:22 (NKJV) states, "The lamp of the body is the eye. If therefore, your eye is good, your whole body will be full of light. But if your eye is bad, your whole body will be full of darkness. If therefore the light that is in you is darkness, how great is that darkness!"[1]

---

1   Matthew 6:22 (NKJV).

CHAPTER 2:

What's in My Mirror?

On Sunday, June 19, 2016, I took off my glasses to see the real me. Short hair with strains of gray and silver. Freckles and moles lingered slightly beneath my eyes. A gentle smirk on my face because I had just finished talking to my sister about our "mirror and Bible" chapter assignments given by our spiritual elder mother, Dr. Sonoma Carney Suggs, PhD. My eyes were tired, with a little puffiness. But what did I see? I'm blessed, I'm thankful and healthy, but tense. What will the God in me reveal? I have a light in me which shines, however, it could use more wattage. Who am I? What is my mission from God on this earth? I am a strong-minded, good person searching for a God-sent love. What is my role? How do I fix the procrastination? Where is my fire and passion for having a business? In an attempt to answer these questions, I've come to realize that I need to work on my posture and learn to smile more often.

Wednesday, June 22, 2016: I have darkness under my left eye as if someone has punched me! Tired eyes, ears a little bigger. I see frown lines forming on my forehead.

Friday, June 24, 2016: I inquired of myself, "What is my 'why' for spiritual growth?" Because I love the feeling and it makes me happy! My hunger for God's word has increased. I then thought, "What is my 'why' for a financial blessing?" So that I may give to church programs helping those in need, provide for my child, decorate my home, buy another car, and increase my donations to organizations like the Navy-Marine Corps Relief Society, Rescue Mission, and food bank centers. Also to help my sister with the upkeep of the family home. What did I learn from this Bible assignment, you might ask? Simply put, no matter what I see in the mirror, I am perfect in God's eyes and created in His image.

"So, God created man in His own image; in the image of God, He created him; male and female He created them."[2]

GENESIS 1:27 [NKJV]

As I continue to study the Holy Bible and observe myself daily in my mirror, this exercise instructs me on how to be a hearer and doer of His word.

"For if anyone is a hearer of the word and not a doer, he is like a man observing his natural face in a mirror; for he observes himself, goes away, and immediately forgets what kind of man he was. But he who looks into the perfect law of liberty and continues in it and is not a forgetful hearer but a doer of the work, this one will be blessed in what he does."[3]

JAMES 1:23–25 [NKJV]

---

2   Genesis 1:27 (NKJV).
3   James 1:23–25 (NKJV).

Fast forward to today. What changed in my mirror? A God-fearing woman who has learned to lift her head yet humbles herself. A God-fearing woman who is incredibly careful of what flows from her mouth after being attacked by hurtful words. A woman now without boasting pride and who is unashamed of loving God.

> **"But we all, with unveiled face, beholding as in a mirror the glory of the Lord, are being transformed into the same image from glory to glory, just as by the Spirit of the Lord."**[4]
>
> 2 CORINTHIANS 3:18 [NKJV]

If you value your salvation, don't be afraid to look in the mirror and ask yourself, "What do you see?" And as you check yourself in that mirror, I also encourage you to check your spirit. How much of God's armor do you have on today? Lamentations 3:40 provides a checklist. Once you have read this scripture, I recommend you start a journal and log what it is you see in yourself. However, before starting your day, just know God created you in His image.

---

4   2 Corinthians 3:18 (NKJV).

CHAPTER 3

Woman With a Past Put Your Junk on the Front Lawn

Momma didn't want me, and daddy made comments under intoxicating drink. "I might not be his," he said. No worries, I'm going to be alright because the Almighty Creator makes no mistakes!

"Everyone who is called by My name, Whom I have created for My glory; I have formed him, yes, I have made him."[5]

ISAIAH 43:7 [NKJV]

During my personal journey of ascending from everlasting destruction to eternal life, I experienced situations that exposed me and made me vulnerable to everyday sin. Seeking change, I had to acknowledge my transgressions. Yes, I had to lift the light-blocking shades of the haunted house in which I dwelled in order to prepare myself for the move of the Holy Spirit. Let me explain. God needed me to move for His purpose. I needed to be evicted out of my old way

---

5   Isaiah 43:7 (NKJV).

of thinking and living and enter into His new way. I had to surrender to the Holy Spirit whom God and Jesus gave authority to pull everything out of the secret closets, the dark places, and the attics of my mind, body, and tormented soul. He then instructed the Landlord, or the Holy Spirit, to serve me with an eviction notice and to put my junk on the front lawn.

As the subject line reveals, this is when I put *some* of my past junk on the front lawn, in transparent boxes for the readers of this book to pick through, examine, and even judge. I'm dumping the next four topics on you early because my prayer is that by the time you finish this book, you will have a better understanding of why it's important to strive and pray for transition and change. In addition, I'd like you to keep in mind that no man comes to the Father, but through His Son, who will judge each of us for our faith and our works. Therefore, acknowledging the truth about my journey sets me free from sin, guilt, and shame. As a child of God, I must be able to hear Him. As the Holy Spirit speaks, I must believe His words. I've often asked myself, "Were my dreams a sign showing how I would learn to walk as a spiritual light of life?" And the answer is yes! It is true. The Holy Spirit revealed it to me. Finally, I will leave you with this message. Don't be quick to accuse, judge, or condemn me for what I have written. Again, this is my truth. It is through spiritual therapy and healing that I no longer walk in darkness. It is what's in my book!

"I am the light of the world. He who follows Me shall not walk in darkness but have the light of life."[6]

JOHN 8:12 [NKJV]

---

6   John 8:12 (NKJV).

BONDAGE

According to the *Merriam-Webster Dictionary (MWD) Online*, bondage is defined as "the tenure or service of a villein, serf, or an enslaved person" or "a state of being bound usually by compulsion (as of law or mastery)"[7] (1). What were my forms of bondage? Drugs, drinking, having a mouth full of cursing and a heart filled with bitterness. This started in my early childhood years, way before I joined the navy. Now, for those who know my family background, alcohol, drugs, and other things, which I'll unveil shortly, were a part of my upbringing. Even today, I may occasionally fall short of God's expectations due to one or two of these bondages. However, because of God's grace, mercy, peace, and the liberty Jesus Christ gives me to be free, those worldly compulsions have subsided drastically. In fact, I refuse to let these sins have dominion over me. I now have the strength, and spiritual-will to overcome those powerful compulsions. With continuous fasting, prayer, and asking God for clarity, I'm destined for a wonderful future because of His power operating in my life. I have a purpose as a messenger for Him.

"**Stand fast therefore in the liberty by which Christ has made us free, and do not be entangled again with a yoke of bondage.**"[8]

GALATIANS 5:1 [NKJV]

MOLESTATION

One morning, after I thanked God and gave Him praise for His grace and mercy, my thoughts detoured and abruptly reminisced about my childhood. Like a wisdom tooth that was never pulled years

---

7   https://www.merriam-webster.com/dictionary/bondage
8   Galatians 5:1 (NKJV).

ago pushing through sensitive gums, one of my most painful memories surfaced out of the darkness of my mind. The vision reminded me of my innocence secretly removed and my childhood altered after being sexually molested by an older male cousin. Making matters worse, I clearly envisioned how other relatives had nicknamed me "the ugly duckling" because I whined all the time (sounding and looking like a baby duck). I believe many of them thought I was just a spoiled kid. I wouldn't call myself spoiled; I was damaged.

Raised in a two-parent home, my father and mother worked demanding jobs to put food on the table. Unfortunately, staying at home to care for me was not an option for my mother back in the sixties. Both of my parents had to be at work at the crack of dawn, while my sister and brother rode the school bus. Monday through Friday my mother would drop me off at the family caretaker's home, and each morning the caretaker took me to kindergarten class. I remember crying and clinging to my mother so she wouldn't leave me. She'd quickly hand me off to the caretaker and speed off to work. I don't remember every finite detail. However, after taking a child development course in college on parenting and "Children's Relationships," I realized some of my adult actions developed from the experience of my childhood innocence being ripped away. An article on Raising Children Network mentions, "Through relationships, your child learns vital information about their world. For example, your child learns whether the world is safe and secure, whether they're loved, who loves them, what happens when they cry or laugh, and much more"[9] (Relationships: the foundation of child development. 2020) (par. 5).

---

9   https://raisingchildren.net.au/newborns/development/understanding-development/development-first-five-years

Fast forward to the year 2018. As I continued to grow my faith in God and study His word, I learned that in order for me to progress from this childhood tragedy which had continued to haunt me, I had to humble myself and forgive, (yes, forgive) the molester, the trusted family caretaker, and most of all, my parents.

One morning, after having another flashback, I got up to shower and start my day. As I was standing under the running water, the thought of my past overwhelmed me so that I began weeping, then profusely crying. With shower water and tears running down my face, I shouted out, "You were supposed to protect me!" and "You all were supposed to protect me!"

After releasing this heavy burden, peace overpowered me as I felt in my soul the Holy Spirit comfort, encourage, and coach me to release the words "I forgive you all in the mighty name of Jesus." On that day, the chain of bondage broke, and I closed that chapter of my book.

Save yourself! Surrender the mental destruction that's been tormenting you all these years. Forgive, repent, and allow the Holy Spirit—"the Helper"—to free you from yourself, and propel you into your blessing of the "right now." Your heavenly life depends on it. Amen and Hallelujah!

HOMOSEXUALITY AND LGBTQ

By this time, I know you're saying, "My goodness, she's really putting her junk out on the front lawn!" Well, for those of you who understand the phrase, "the struggle is real," I present to you one more box. It's loaded with the very controversial topic of homosexuality and LGBTQ. The sharp views and opinions of this lifestyle divide countries, families, and religions all around the world. Now, if you're turning up your nose, shaking your head, or you're looking for the biggest stone to throw, take a deep breath, pick up your Bible, and let's walk through this together.

I would like to address three questions. First, what is man's definition of homosexuality and LGBTQ? Second, is the word "homosexuality" anywhere in the Bible? If not, why use the word "abomination" to describe such an act? Third, is this sin an automatic deal-breaker for living an eternal life with God? I specifically address the second and third questions to "men and women of the cloth" who boldly profess themselves true appointed and anointed shepherds of God's sheep. I'll address this statement shortly.

What is homosexuality? During my research, I found and chose Encyclopedia Britannica's meaning (written by man) which states that homosexuality is "the sexual interest in and attraction to members of one's own sex"[10] (par. 1). Am I guilty and have I taken part in this sinful behavior? Yes! Remember, I'm putting my junk on the front lawn, and this is what's in my book. When society and religious groups categorize individuals who identify themselves as lesbian, gay, bisexual, transgender, and/or queer (LGBTQ), they see sinners who are not normal going through a phase or need transforming through therapy, prayer, and anointing with oil. In fact, the seriousness of having a desire for or attraction to someone of the same sex has increased in debates, studies, and law over the years. Some psychologists have classified it as a mental illness. In my case, I honestly can't explain how it happened. Is it because of my childhood trauma, or is it a generational curse? Again, God makes no mistakes.

---

10   https://www.britannica.com/topic/homosexuality

But He allows us to choose right from wrong. Therefore, it's imperative I choose to follow God's word and not walk in darkness.

Before I address the second question, I'm going to ask you to secure your spiritual vessel for rough seas. Ready? Pick up your Bible, and let's dive into the word. As I flip through the pages from front to back—books, chapters, verses, and even the concordance—nowhere in the Bible could I find the word "homosexuality," "gay," "lesbian," etc. However, so many of God's shepherds (men and women) use these "man-made" words to scoff at those who today or in the past identified with this sin. (For those of you who have read this far, notice I'm acknowledging this is a sin). What these proclaimed shepherds of God—apostles, prophets, preachers, teachers, etc.—normally do is associate the word "homosexuality" with the word "abomination."

Theologian professors may have quizzed their students with the following question: "What language did the word 'abomination' originate from?" Research shows it came from the Hebrew Bible terms *shiqquts* and *sheqets*. These words describe someone or something that is detested. The Latin term *abominari* means "to deprecate as an ill omen." However, the English term "abomination" means wicked, vile, sinful, hateful, or even loathsome.

In researching for the meaning of God's word "abomination," there's a whole slew of laws dealing with sexual immorality and how one can defile themselves by breaking the laws found in the Old Testament (Leviticus 18:22, 20:13) and New Testament (Romans 1:27), to name a few. I present this statement to individuals who claim they are God's appointed messenger. Those individuals who use sermons or teachings about homosexuality to scare, condemn, and pre-judge may cause themselves to be judged harshly by God. You may ask, "How?" Well, when you tell someone "they're going to burn in Hell" for this sin, you (proclaimed Shepherd of God) have now placed judgment against them (God's sheep), which you don't have the authority to do. God has the final say! I ask you to take a deep breath before you answer the following question. Are you now walking the fine line between being a "scoffer" and "mocker" as described in the book of Jude (1:16–19)? Are your harsh teachings causing sinners to repent or rebel?

> **"The devising of foolishness is sin, And the scoffer is an abomination to men."**[11]
>
> **PROVERBS 24:9 [NKJV]**

The third question is "Is this sin an automatic deal-breaker for eternal life with God?" Again, there's no passage found proving homosexuality is an "automatic" one-way ticket on a bullet train to eternal damnation or everlasting punishment. However, I highly encourage the people, specifically men, of this community to read Deuteronomy 23:1 (KJV). So, is taking part in homosexuality behavior a sin? Yes! Is it wicked? Indeed. Is it one of the Lord's seven hated abominations listed in Proverbs (6:16–19 NKJV)? No! Therefore, everyone, especially men and women of the cloth, should be careful not to add to His word. Prevent yourself from being "a lying tongue" (v.17). Turn your mirror around, ask God to forgive you for leading His sheep astray, and repent from being "a false witness who speaks lies, and one who sows discord among brethren." (v.19)

---

11   Proverbs 24:9 (NKJV).

In conclusion, for those of us who confess "the struggle is real," just know God sent His only begotten Son to die for our sins. Don't allow others to deceive you about this sin and do not deceive yourself. Continue to strive for righteousness!

> "If we say that we have no sin, we deceive ourselves, and the truth is not in us. If we confess our sins, He is faithful and just to forgive us our sins and to cleanse us from all unrighteousness."[12]
>
> 1 JOHN 1:8–9 [NKJV]

ADULTERY AND DIVORCE

The definition of adultery, according to the Oxford University Press, is "voluntary sexual intercourse between a married person and a person who is not his or her spouse" (Press 2021). Guilty? Yes! Again, let me remind you, this is in my book. The top songs of my adultery playlist were Shirley Murdock's "As We Lay," Jonathan Butler's "More Than Just Friends," Carl Thomas' "Wish I Never Met Her," John Legend's "She Don't Have To Know" and the list goes on.

Thank God for growth, spiritual guidance, and the ability to repent and ask for forgiveness for my sins. Putting my past on the front lawn, I'm amazed and embarrassed about the motto I had as a young sailor in my twenties and thirties. It went something like this: "I'm a married person's nightmare!" What did this mean? I would have my fun with someone else's spouse because there was no commitment. When the relationship got complicated, I would tell them, "Go home to your family." (If you've been on either side of adultery; acting as the criminal or the victim, stop, and take a deep breath.)

---

12   1 John 1:8–9 (NKJV).

Remember the Bible study mirror assignment from the last chapter? This occurred many years after I honorably discharged from the navy. My spiritual mother, Dr. Sonoma Carney Suggs, gave me a prophetic reality check. It blew me away when she assigned to me the topic of "adultery." After researching and studying God's word, my distasteful motto was heartless and the words of a young woman once wild were regretful. Looking back in my mirror, I put myself in the spouse's shoes. The shame of the sin was overwhelming.

The Seventh Commandment:
"You shall not commit adultery."[13]
EXODUS 20:14 [NKJV]

The history of divorce is also a very controversial Bible topic in every earthly religion, just like homosexuality and adultery. When two people join in a marriage not put together by God, dissolve the marriage by divorce, and step into a new marriage, each unique situation often causes heated debates among Christians. So, here's another fact about me. I got married in my fifties. One year and about six months later, I filed for divorce from my husband. It was not because of sexual immorality or fornication. We departed using man's law known as "Marital Dissolution Agreement."

Now, what does God's law state? Let's start with the Book of Matthew 5:31–32 (NKJV). It explains how a husband will cause his wife to commit adultery when he gives her a certificate of divorce for anything other than sexual immorality or fornication. I honor God's written word. Therefore, I choose not to add anything to these scriptures, nor take any of His words away. At present, my ex-husband

---

13   Exodus 20:14 (NKJV).

still lives. Hence, my adultery "get out of jail pass" is revoked. Thank You, Christ Jesus, for wisdom and understanding! For now, a new marriage will have to wait.

Many of you may not agree with what you just read. Guess what? That's alright with me. In fact, here's one more Bible verse for you to ponder over concerning divorce:

> "Now to the married I command, yet not I but the Lord:
> A wife is not to depart from her husband. But even if she does
> depart, let her remain unmarried or be reconciled to her husband.
> And a husband is not to divorce his wife."[14]
>
> 1 CORINTHIANS 7:10–11 [NKJV]

Again, what does this mean for me? Well, my son would jokingly console me by saying, "Mom, just be happy with Jesus alone." Under the circumstances, that's good advice.

Listen, we all make mistakes. It's important that we recognize, learn, acknowledge, repent, and change from our sinful ways. We can identify adultery and divorce as a cause-and-effect relationship. If you are currently experiencing either situation, don't allow pride to fuel the fire. Stop the disrespect, flirting, enticing, or even provoking comments. If you think about it and have a strong desire in your heart for it, you've already sinned. Let your conscience be your guide. "Go and Sin No More"! Finally, as we go through this journey together and with the help of the Holy Spirit, we will discover "how to ascend from everlasting destruction to eternal life!"

---

14   1 Corinthians 7:10–11 (NKJV).

CHAPTER 4

Spirit-Mind Connection
and Renewal

In the weight training world, there's a scientific program called "mind-muscle connection" in which bodybuilders use their mind to improve the quality of muscle fibers by focusing on a specific part of the body (i.e., arms, chest, etc.). As believers of God, we too can use this concept with the help of spiritual meditation and prayer, reading the word, and guarding what we allow in our eye and ear gates, which connect to our mind and heart. We can all start by meditating on these questions from the Lord in Job 38:36 (NKJV), where He asked, "Who has put wisdom in the mind? Or who has given understanding to the heart?"[15]

If you turn off the many reprobate distractions of television, magazines, social media, and technology and allow yourself to decrease stress and get in a quiet place, you will experience the comfort and reward with spirit-filled mental peace and a connection to the Holy Spirit. Find time for peace even if it's only a few minutes a day.

---

15   Job 38:36 (NKJV).

> "You will keep him in perfect peace. Whose mind is
> stayed on You. Because he trusts in You."[16]
>
> ISAIAH 26:3 [NKJV]

Once you have created a daily workout routine for your spirit-mind, God will give you specific instructions on how to develop this necessary and powerful muscle. "And do not be conformed to this world, but be transformed by the renewing of your mind, that you may prove what is that good and acceptable and perfect will of God"[17] (Romans 12:2 [NKJV]).

The previous scripture is important, especially in today's society of increasing classifications of mental health disorders. Categories such as substance-related disorders, mood and anxiety disorders, and Post-Traumatic Syndrome Disorder (PTSD) are all causing individuals to seek therapy from man. As I continue to ascend and transition away from negative areas of emotional conflict in my life, it's comforting to know my best defense mechanism is God. He is my therapist and psychiatrist.

> "... and be renewed in the spirit of your mind and
> that you put on the new man which was created according
> to God, in true righteousness and holiness."[18]
>
> EPHESIANS 4:23–24 [NKJV]

Finally, to lighten things up a bit, I'd like to leave you with a thought-provoking thought to debate with family and friends about the human mind.

---

16   Isaiah 26:3 (NKJV).
17   Romans 12:2 (NKJV).
18   Ephesians 4:23–24 (NKJV).

As described earlier in the book, my occupation in the navy was a yeoman. In case you forgot, it's an office manager or administrator, jack of all trades on steroids. The sailors whose jobs were more physical, strenuous, and hands-on, would make jokes, saying, "The only thing a yeoman does is sit at a desk and push paper all day. Your medical emergency would comprise a paper cut." However, my sincere response would start like this: "You use your body muscles to complete your job. When you get tired, you drink water, an energy drink, or a strong cup of navy coffee to revive and replenish yourself. The mind is still functioning. However, as a person whose job is the constant and repetitive use of the mind, when it gets tired, not only does it stop functioning properly, but it also takes the entire body with it." What am I saying? "When the mind depletes itself and shuts down, the body will soon follow."

In conclusion, exercise your spirit-mind with the word of God to keep it righteous, renewed, and sound. Seek Bible scriptures such as 2 Timothy 1:7 (NKJV) which says, "For God has not given us a spirit of fear, but of power and of love and of a sound mind."[19]

19   2 Timothy 1:7 (NKJV).

CHAPTER 5

Fasting and Prayer

What does it mean to fast? According to the *MWD Online,* (for us old-school folk), it means "to abstain from food" or "to eat sparingly or abstain from some foods."[20] The King James Version (KJV) dictionary (av1611) defines the word as "to abstain from food, beyond the usual time; to omit to take the usual meals, for a time; as to fast a day or a week."[21]

The Hebrew word for "fast" is *Tsoom,* which means to cover over. And the Greek word is *nace tyoo-o,* which means to abstain. Now, here are a couple of mind-tingling questions. First, do you believe you should fast and pray? If you agree, then you're already on the right track. Second, do God and Christ Jesus expect us to fast? Again, if your answer is "yes," you're batting two for two. Dust off your Bible, open Matthew 6:16–18 and read. Pay close attention to the key word, "when."

---

20   https://www.merriam-webster.com/dictionary/fast
21   King James Version (KJV) Dictionary.

Now, why should a Christian, or those of you who are on the fence about your faith and belief, dedicate yourself to fasting and prayer?

Here are five reasons:

1. To know God's Will

2. To seek God's face more fully and to receive a more intimate relationship with the Holy Spirit

3. For humility and repentance

4. To develop discipline

5. To ask God for something you desire

Alright, next, let's explore seven ways of fasting

1. Single fasting – meaning private or alone

2. Marital fasting – described in (1 Corinthians 7:5 NKJV) by the Apostle Paul

3. Group fasting – promoted by churches and organizations to bring in the New Year

4. Intermittent fasting – normally lasts a few hours, a day, or several days

5. Longer fasting – week or more

6. Water-only fasting

7. No food or water – Amen

If we want to follow in Jesus' footsteps, then we must do our best to emulate Him. So, did Jesus fast? and if He did, why? Matthew 4:1–2 (NKJV) states:

"Then Jesus was led up by the Spirit into the wilderness to be tempted by the devil. And when He had fasted 40 days and 40 nights, afterward He was hungry."[22] Now we have knowledge of Jesus Christ's fasting.

Luke 4:1–2 (NKJV) shows, "Then Jesus, being filled with the Holy Spirit, returned from the Jordan, and was led by the Spirit into the wilderness, 2) being tempted for forty days by the devil. And in those days, He ate nothing, and afterward, when they had ended, He was Hungry."[23]

Fasting and prayer allow us to humble ourselves and please our Lord. It also strengthens our flesh against the wills and desires of the evil one. However, is it possible we can fast and pray the wrong way, for the wrong reason, and for the wrong things? The answer to this question is "yes." We are often guilty of going before the Father in the flesh and not surrendering our soul.

"Is it a fast that I have chosen, a day for a man to afflict his soul?
Is it to bow down his head like a bulrush, and to spread out
sackcloth and ashes? Would you call this a fast,
and an acceptable day to the Lord?"[24]

ISAIAH 58:5 [NKJV]

---

22   Matthew 4:1–2 (NKJV).
23   Luke 4:1–2 (NKJV).
24   Isaiah 58:5 (NKJV).

In case you missed it, Christ had to be filled with the Holy Spirit through His fasting. Therefore, when you fast, do it to seek understanding, clarity, and for God. Don't fast just to follow the crowd.

The most popular fast from the Bible, more so than any other, is the Daniel Fast. When you Google search or YouTube this specific fast, a multitude of information will appear.

Daniel and his men sacrificed not eating certain foods of the King Nebuchadnezzar. They did not want to defile themselves. This is a perfect example of why we should detox our bodies or temples, especially with what we consume today. If we want to be renewed, restored, and rewarded by Christ Jesus and God, we must fast and pray.

> **"So, Daniel said to the steward whom the chief of the**
> **eunuchs had set over Daniel, Hananiah, Mishaal, and Azariah,**
> **'Please test your servants for ten days, and let them give us**
> **vegetables to eat and water to drink.'"** [25]
>
> DANIEL 1:11–12 [NKJV]

> **"And at the end of ten days, their features appeared**
> **better and fatter in flesh than all the young men who**
> **ate the portion of the king's delicacies."** [26]
>
> DANIEL 1:15 [NKJV]

Daniel, Hananiah, Mishaal, and Azariah chose to Fast and not defile themselves. God rewarded them with favor and goodwill. (See Daniel 1:17 NKJV). If you are serious about this transition from

---

25   Daniel 1:11–12 (NKJV).
26   Daniel 1:15 (NKJV).

everlasting destruction to eternal life, you must pass the fast and pray test.

In conclusion, fasting and prayer are difficult, but they are necessities. You will have many distractions and temptations. However, when you lose focus, think about the sacrifice Jesus Christ made for us. What you give up for a few days is nothing compared to what He gave us. Start your sacrifice today and remember "when" you fast and pray, you are walking further away from everlasting darkness and into a brighter light. And if you really want to be more like Jesus Christ, be prepared to sacrifice!

CHAPTER 6:

Listen With a Spiritual Ear

Today's society is teaching us to listen carefully to those who pique our interest. But what does it mean to listen? According to the *MWD Online,* to listen is "to hear something with thoughtful attention."[27] Humanity inundates the world with positive words of inspirations, such as love, working together, sharing, and connecting. In contrast, there's an overwhelming abundance of negative fuel tossed into the fire with words like hatred, noncooperation, selfishness, and unprecedented separation and division. Modern technology, which has been a blessing to some and a curse for others, contributes to what we pay attention to and hear. What's the big deal? Well, if you're not careful of what you allow in your ear gates, this might lead to your ultimate demise.

Referring to the Bible, we find that having a deaf ear to God's word, or not having a willingness to hear His word, has caused humankind's trouble from the very beginning of time. This occurs when our spiritual ear encounters evil frequencies, which turns the truth into a lie. This concept alone should cause you to tremble.

---

27   Merriam-Webster.com Thesaurus, s.v. "listen".

For example, when Jesus was speaking to Abraham's descendants, followers of Satan, they did not care to listen or hear that Jesus Christ was the Son of God.

> **"Why do you not understand my speech?**
> **Because you are not able to listen to My word."[28]**
>
> JOHN 8:43 [NKJV]

Here's something else to consider about listening to God and the messengers He sends on His behalf. If you don't fear Him or hear His words, you will miss your blessing of understanding God's wisdom and knowledge. Proverbs 1:7, 33 (NKJV) gives two examples stating,

> **"The fear of the Lord is the beginning of knowledge,**
> **but fools despise wisdom and instruction."**
>
> (V. 7)

> **"But whoever listens to me will dwell safely,**
> **and will be secure, without fear of evil."[29]**
>
> (V. 33)

The spiritual ear allows you to listen and hear all the good things sent down by God. However, in contrast, the worldly ears will betray you. In fact, if not careful, what you hear may be instructions from other spirits, like a lover of yourself or the spirit of fallen angels.

---

28   John 8:43 (NKJV).
29   Proverbs 1:7, 33 (NKJV).

Not knowing the difference will cause you to develop foolish beliefs which are not of God.

> "For the time will come when they will not endure sound doctrine, but according to their own desires, because they have itching ears, they will heap up for themselves teachers; and they will turn their ears away from the truth and be turned aside to fables."[30]
>
> 2 TIMOTHY 4:3–4 [NKJV]

What does all this hoopla about listening with your spiritual ear boil down to? You must prepare yourself for the inevitable return of Jesus Christ. If you don't remember anything else from this chapter, or don't read another page in this book, highlight these next two verses from the book of Revelation. It's imperative we get this work assignment checked off in the judgment book. Our eternal life depends on it!

> "Blessed is he who reads and those who hear the words of this prophecy and keep those things which are written in it; for the time is near."[31]
>
> REVELATION 1:3 [NKJV]

> "He who has an ear, let him hear what the Spirit says to the churches. To him who overcomes I will give to eat from the tree of life, which is in the midst of the Paradise of God."[32]
>
> REVELATION 2:7 [NKJV]

---

30   2 Timothy 4:3–4 (NKJV).
31   Revelation 1:3 (NKJV).
32   Revelation 2:7 (NKJV).

Finally, I'd like to leave you with this profound quote taken from a young man named Jerod Smith: "The ability to hear God's voice is for everyone. All you must do is ask Him. Stop depending on others to hear for you"[33] (Identity and Purpose Summit, 2021).

Understand, the Holy Ghost will help us ask anything according to God's will and teach us to hear God's voice. God's Son, Jesus Christ, will petition His Father to listen to our desires.

---

33   "Identity and Purpose Summit | Dr. Faith."

CHAPTER 7

Let the Lord Lead

W‌hat does the word "lead" mean to you? While you're trying to answer, let's first examine the definitions of the word.

According to the Oxford University Press (OUP), the verb form of lead means "to cause (a person or animal) to go with one by holding them by the hand, a halter, a rope, etc. while moving forward."[34] Other frequently used words or terms are guide, conduct, show, usher, escort, steer, pilot, marshal. A notable connected to "lead" is "shepherd." I'll discuss this specific word more in depth shortly.

In its noun form, lead means "a route or means of access to a particular place or in a particular direction." For example, when you go to a restaurant or concert, someone will lead you to your table or seat. Lead can also mean "the initiative in an action; an example for others." In addition, when used as a synonym, it means forefront, superiority, or first position. Individuals such as our parents, presidents, CEOs, or commanding officers fall into these categories.

---

34   https://www.lexico.com/en/definition/lead

Now, let's go back to school a little more and I want to cover the five "Ws": who, what, when, where, and why when referencing "let the Lord lead."

Previously, I mentioned the word shepherd. Sticking with what's in my book, it's important that I recognize who is leading me from everlasting destruction to eternal life. So, you may ask, "WHO is your leading shepherd?" Well, the Lord is my shepherd.

> **"The Lord is my shepherd; I shall not want.**
> **He makes me to lie down in green pastures; He leads me**
> **beside the still waters. He restores my soul; He leads me in**
> **the paths of righteousness For His name's sake ..."[35]**
>
> PSALM 23:1−4 [KNJV]

Reiterating the latter scripture, the Lord is my heavenly Shepherd, with the help of the Holy Spirit, who leads me from day to day.

When you become a devoted member of a church organization and fellowship under a religious leader, he or she acts as your earthly shepherd. He or she spiritually guides, nurtures, and teaches you through scripture, prayer, worship, counseling, etc.

Our Lord, with the help of the Holy Spirit, and our earthly shepherds, steer, guide, and move us forward spiritually. All are watching over us, providing the love and care we need to follow in Jesus' footsteps.

---

35   Psalm 23:1−4 (NKJV).

WHAT happens when we allow the Lord (our heavenly Shepherd) to lead us?

As I previously mentioned, we move forward and upward spiritually, and He steers us in the right direction. Because the Lord leads us, we will not go astray. He protects us.

WHEN faced with temptation, our Lord will help guide us from it. Where trouble leads us, He will take us by the hand and steer us from evil. Our heavenly Shepherd restores us and puts us on the paths of righteousness, according to Psalm 23:3 (KNJV).

As the end time draws near, we don't want to be on the path of destruction or eternal damnation. I fully agree that God the Father, the Son, and the Holy Spirit cannot lie. They are faithful, merciful, and true.

If you've read this far, but still consider yourself to be a sinner, this is an opportunity to repent and receive God as your personal Savior through His Son and the Holy Spirit.

Act today by declaring these words:

"Show me Your ways, O Lord; Teach me Your paths.
Lead me in Your truth and teach me, for You are the God
of my salvation; On You I wait all the day."[36]

PSALM 25:4–5 [KNJV]

As your faith in God continues to grow, you don't want someone or something that is spiritually blind leading you. It could be your spouse, partner, family, friends, or even the astonishingly

---

36   Psalm 25:4–5 (NKJV).

intelligent technology developed today. Speaking of technology, it has overwhelmed the church body and stepped up its game in spiritual leader deception. It has placed a dark blanket over mankind's eyes and promised it will lead us into the future faster with greater health, wealth, fantasy, and prosperity. When in fact, modern technology is leading believers and sinners by the hand to everlasting damnation. A perfect example is the worldwide use of Meta (previously known as Facebook). Created and developed by a young man with the powerful ability to see into the future, his invention has proven to be positive, fruitful, good, and evil. For instance, family and friends have reconnected. Small towns unveiled locally thriving businesses, thus increasing their sales and finances. It created new millionaires daily because of their telecommunication success. We can stay in our pj's while visually traveling the world without leaving home. However, as mankind's need for speed, greed, power, and authority develops, again this type of technology has and will also increase its spread of demonic, mind-altering tactics.

With the push of a button, we are quickly losing the use of our God-given senses to discern right from wrong, worship, and communicate with each other, thus removing the human spiritual connection. But Jesus Christ gives us specific instructions on how to handle such a situation.

"Let them alone. They are blind leaders of the blind. And if the blind leads the blind, both will fall into a ditch."[37]

MATTHEW 15:14 [NKJV]

---

37   Matthew 15:14 (NKJV).

Therefore, we must make good, sound choices to let the Lord lead us. A saying in the military goes like this: "Pay attention to detail." Don't allow worldly idols, false prophets, and spiritual counterfeits to blind you.

Finally, WHY should we allow the Lord to lead us? I have listed three important eternal life reasons:

1. Because He is our Shepherd, and we are the sheep.

2. He keeps us from being led astray and down the wide and crooked path.

3. As sheep, we need the Lord to lead and guide us to green pastures and still waters where we can eat, drink, and feast on His Holy Word.

GIVE YOUR LIFE TO JESUS TODAY
AND LET THE LORD LEAD YOU!

CHAPTER 8:

Follow the Lord

If you are at a point in your life where you have been baptized with water in the name of the Father, and the Son, and Holy Spirit, I commend you for giving your life to Jesus Christ and accepting Him as your personal Savior. Now you're wondering what happens next. Well, I'd like to present to you a spiritual plan or starter kit explaining how to follow the Lord.

Most people believe "If I'm letting Him lead me, I should just follow Him and that's it." As simple as it sounds, there are those who truly don't know how to follow Him without specific instructions, a guide, directions, or a map. It's like learning to march with your military company. Each individual must follow the person in front of them in order to march in step. In addition, there's a "guidon" who holds the company flag, the cadence caller who reminds you what boot to put down, and the Company Commander (CC) who will definitely chasten you when you're not following directions. Therefore, allow me to analyze the word "follow" and then guide you to the Bible for further instructions concerning following our Lord and Savior Jesus Christ.

Breaking it down in a church school fashion, OUP defines "follow" as to "go or come after (a person or thing proceeding ahead); move or travel behind."[38]

Phrases such as "come after," "go after," and "on the heels of" are synonyms of follow. Now, of the previously listed synonyms, I'd like to focus on the example of "come after." Mark 8:34 (NKJV) states, "When He had called the people to Himself, with His disciples also, He said to them, 'Whoever desires to come after Me, let him deny himself, and take up his cross, and follow Me.'"[39]

The King James Version (KJV) dictionary uses terms like:

1. To pursue or to pursue with the eye

2. To chase

3. To accompany

According to OUP, the word "accompany" means to "go somewhere with (someone) as a companion or escort."

> "As Jesus passed on from there, He saw a man named Matthew sitting at the tax office. And He said to him, "Follow Me." So, he arose and followed Him."[40]
>
> MATTHEW 9:9 [NKJV]

In this scripture, Jesus gave Matthew an instruction. He desired to follow Jesus, and he became a companion of Jesus. Amen!

---

38   https://www.lexico.com/en/definition/follow
39   Mark 8:34 (NKJV).
40   Matthew 9:9 (NKJV).

Digging deeper into the power of the word "follow," another definition describes it as taking action. In other words, it means "to imitate, to copy, to obey, to practice; to act in conformity to."

"Therefore, be imitators of God as dear children. 2. And walk in love, as Christ also has loved us and given Himself for us, an offering, and a sacrifice to God for a sweet-smelling aroma."[41]

EPHESIANS 5:1–2 [NKJV]

As a witness and messenger, I can honestly say, following the Lord will help you walk in love and become a sacrifice to God.

When talking about conformity, compliance with standards, rules, or laws, it's imperative that I educate you in the laws that all men, not only Christians, must follow to prepare for God's eternal judgment. Therefore, you must concern yourself with what's written and documented in your book! As Christians following the Lord, it is our duty to adhere to and practice the commands of the Lord. Why? Because that is a blessing! Here's how we receive another blessing for following and imitating the Lord.

"Then Jesus spoke to them again saying, 'I am the light of the world. He who follows Me shall not walk in darkness but have the light of life'."[42]

JOHN 8:12 [NKJV]

When in the Body of Christ, whether you are a part of the Five-Fold Ministry or another denomination, again, it's imperative you

---

41   Ephesians 5:1–2 (NKJV).
42   John 8:12 (NKJV).

understand that following the Lord will not always be comfortable. Hold on to your seatbelt because following Him will cause suffering. Wait! Don't close the book yet. I'll explain. But first, remember I talked about how an earthly shepherd should lead you? Well, if your earthly shepherd during his or her tenure, has never addressed the mere fact that you will, at one point or another, suffer persecution by following Christ Jesus, consider this as a red flag. When the earthly shepherd you follow only speaks of joy, prosperity, manifestation, and vows to you about not suffering, be worried. In fact, in 1 Peter 2:20–21 (NKJV), Apostle Peter states, "For what credit is it, when you are beaten for your faults, you take it patiently? But, when you do good and suffer, if you take it patiently, this is commendable before God. For to this you were called because Christ also suffered for us, leaving us an example, that you should follow His steps:"[43]

However harsh, be prepared to suffer. You should follow Him as an obedient servant follows the directions of their master. And He is our Master. Note: Moses followed God, Joshua followed Moses, and Caleb followed Joshua. All were obedient servants and perfect examples of individuals who understood the importance of how to follow.

"Nevertheless, my brethren who went up with me made the heart of the people melt, but I wholly followed the Lord my God. So, Moses swore on that day, saying, 'Surely the land where your foot has trodden shall be your inheritance and your children's forever, because you have wholly followed the Lord my God'."[44]

JOSHUA 14:8–9 [NKJV]

---

43   1 Peter 2:20–21 (NKJV).

44   Joshua 14:8–9 (NKJV).

The last sentence of the Bible verse provides hope for generational mantles. Thus, following and being obedient to the Lord will cause a domino effect. Not only are we rewarded as individuals, but our children will also reap the reward of inheritance. So, we're not just following Him, obeying Him, and conforming to His commands for ourselves, but we also must do this for our children and our children's children. Amen!

As followers of the Lord, we agree to adhere, honor, worship, and to serve. Once again, when we follow Jesus as dutiful servants, His Father will honor us.

> "If anyone serves Me, let him follow Me;
> and where I am, there My servant will be also.
> If anyone serves Me, him My Father will honor."[45]
>
> JOHN 12:26 [NKJV]

In conclusion, we should remember and take action to imitate, copy, and obey the Lord and practice acting in conformity with His commands. For after death, when we are standing before God with our book open to be judged, we want it written in our book that we followed the Lord.

> "Blessed are the dead who die in the Lord from now on.' 'that they
> may rest from their labors, and their works follow them'."[46]
>
> REVELATION 14:13 [NKJV]

CONTINUE TO FOLLOW THE LORD!

---

45   John 12:26 (NKJV).
46   Revelation 14:13 (NKJV).

CHAPTER 9:

Abraham's Seed?

I n November, we focus on gathering and spending time with family. We also associate November with food and thanksgiving. Well, today, I'd like us to focus on two words: family and seed. First, let's look at the word "family."

According to the *MWD Online*, family is a social group made up of parents and their children or "a group of persons who come from the same ancestor" (*Thesaurus, par. 1*).

Britannica defines family as "a group of persons united by the ties of marriage, blood, or adoption, constituting a single household, and interacting with each other in their respective social positions, usually those of spouses, parents, children, and siblings."[47]

The Bible discusses family in the very first book. Those of us who believe, understand that Adam and Eve were the mother and father of man. Through generations of procreation, Abram received a promise that you and I benefit from still today. As I write, I feel in my spirit some of you are skeptical. Great! Get your Bible and turn

47   Britannica, T. Editors of Encyclopedia. "family."

to Genesis 12:3 (NKJV). It says, "I will bless those who bless you, and I will curse him who curses you. And in you all the families of the earth shall be blessed."[48]

To whom was God speaking? Abram, whose name will later change to Abraham. Still confused? Look at the part in Genesis 12:3 where God tells Abram, "In you all the families of the earth shall be blessed." It doesn't matter your color, creed, or nationality. God blesses you because of your existence through the seed of Abram right here on earth and not on Mars, Venus, or Jupiter. You are a descendant of the promise. Amen. Here's another verse:

"You are sons of the prophets, and of the covenant which God made with our fathers, saying to Abraham, 'And in your seed all the families of the earth shall be blessed'."[49]

ACTS 3:25 [NKJV]

Alright, what does it mean to be the seed of something or someone? Let's break down the definitions of three types of seed.

1. First type of seed – a flowering plant's units of reproduction, capable of developing into another such plant

2. Second type of seed – a human being

3. Third type of seed – the promise from God concerning the covenant with Abram for his descendants and heirs

---

48   Genesis 12:3 (NKJV).
49   Acts 3:25 (NKJV).

Today, advanced studies have proven how we biologically connect to ancestors going back thousands of years. But you may ask, "How are we connected to Abraham?"

"Just as Abraham believed God, and it was accounted
to him for righteousness. Therefore, know that only those
who are of faith are sons of Abraham."[50]

GALATIANS 3:6–7 [NKJV]

The last sentence poses a question that only you can answer: are you of faith? I pray your answer is "Yes!"

In the New Testament, we learn in order to be justified by faith, we must acknowledge there is only one source, being, or Spirit connecting us to Abraham's seed. His name is Jesus Christ. And He was a seed of Abraham through the seed of David.

"Now to Abraham and his seed were the promises made.
He does not say, 'And the seeds' as of many, but as of one.
'And to your Seed,' who is Christ'."[51]

GALATIANS 3:16 [NKJV]

Finally, here is how we know we are a part of Abraham's family and seed.

---

50   Galatians 3:6–7 (NKJV).
51   Galatians 3:16 (NKJV).

"For you are all sons of God through faith in Christ Jesus.
For as many of you as were baptized into Christ have put on Christ.
There is neither Jew nor Greek, there is neither slave nor free,
there is neither male nor female; for you are all one in Christ Jesus.
And if you are Christ's, then you are Abraham's seed,
and heirs according to the promise."[52]

GALATIANS 3:26-29 [NKJV]

To sum it up, I need you to get excited knowing we are all a part of Abraham's family created by God. However, if you believe there is some skepticism about what's in my book, and you disagree with the writing, know that God will allow you to choose your family in the last days. There's only going to be two. The family of everlasting destruction or the family of eternal life. You choose.

52 Galatians 3:26–29 (NKJV).

CHAPTER 10:

God Gives Us a Choice

G od will not stop the spirit of darkness from tempting you. It's up to you to rebuke sinful temptations and use your faith and love in the Lord and your deliverance to overcome whatever sinful desire you may be facing. It's your choice. For example, as written in the book of Deuteronomy 30:19–20 (NKJV), Moses speaks the words commanded by the Lord to all Israel and states, "I call heaven and earth as witnesses today against you, that I have set before you life and death, blessing and cursing; therefore, choose life, that both you and your descendants may live; that you may love the Lord your God, that you may obey His voice, and that you may cling to Him, for He is your life and the length of your days; and that you may dwell in the land which the Lord swore to your fathers, to Abraham, Isaac, and Jacob, to give them."[53]

When Yah (God) created me in my mother's womb, He chose me to survive and live. In addition, He created me to pursue the assigned destiny and purpose He specifically planned just for me. However, in order to accept the responsibility of His plans, I must

---

53   Deuteronomy 30:19–20 (NKJV).

choose God the Father, the Son, and the Holy Spirit. I can't, nor do I choose to have one without the other. It's an honor, privilege, and blessing knowing They chose me. Thus, I must be obedient and be a faithful yeoman for God.

"You did not choose Me, but I chose you and appointed you that you should go and bear fruit, and that your fruit should remain, that whatever you ask the Father in My name He may give you."[54]

JOHN 15:16 [NKJV]

But wait. There must be a sacrifice when Christ Jesus chooses us to become a messenger or vessel for Him, and it entails suffering or sometimes longsuffering. For example, the Bible tells the story of Saul, a known murderer against early disciples of the Lord. Many feared him. Jesus Christ knew of Saul's destructive behavior but chose him for His purpose. The suffering happened when Jesus Christ blinded Saul by a light from heaven. His blindness put him at the mercy of the very people who feared him. But because Jesus needed Saul (also known as Paul) to speak in His name, Saul converted and followed the instructions given unto him. However, this is what the Lord said to Ananias concerning Saul: "Go thy way: for he is a chosen vessel unto me, to bear my name before the Gentiles, and kings, and the children of Israel: 'For I will shew him how great (many) things he must suffer for my name's sake'"[55] (Acts 9:15–16 [KJV]).

In the book of Romans, Chapter 1, the Apostle Paul goes to Rome to preach the gospel of God. While there, Apostle Paul speaks with the Jews and Greeks about knowing the true will of God. He

---

54 John 15:16 (NKJV).
55 Acts 9:15–16 (KJV).

also teaches the importance of having wisdom and knowledge of His attributes and eternal power. And although they knew right from wrong according to God's word, they indulged in every thinkable sin. They chose the outcome of their destiny.

Today, those sins described in Romans 1:24–32 have multiplied in uncleanness because of wicked spirits and demonic principalities. In fact, the world glorifies, promotes, and worships unrighteousness in everything we see, say, and do. Unless you live on a remote, uninhabited island or in a cave without satellite connection, it is impossible to prevent the daily evil absorbed by our eye and ear gates. Lies, disfiguring of the body, inventions of evil things, disobeying one's parents, unloving spirits, etc. are all corrupt and inexcusable practices. However, there is another choice, and that is to know the righteousness of God. Again, if you choose and accept Yah/God/our heavenly Father, He has already, from the beginning of life, chosen you.

"Just as He chose us in Him before the foundation of the world,
that we should be holy and without blame before Him in love,
having predestined us to adoption as sons by Jesus Christ, to
Himself, according to the good pleasure of the glory of His will."[56]

EPHESIANS 1:4 [NKJV]

Do you believe the Son of God is returning soon? Are you ready for His return? Do you understand He's not coming back with hugs and kisses but with a sharp two-edged sword? If you disagree with the last three questions, beloved, you have a problem. Remember, He gives us a choice. Receive Him in your heart today. Amen!

---

56   Ephesians 1:4 (NKJV).

THOU SHALT NOT KILL FOR BEANS AND RICE

By Laura Elizabeth Watkins

Time is running out. The Earth is showing signs of the end.

Plagues, famine, destruction and death, the world inundated
with sin —

Earthquakes, hail, floods, fire, and winds are knocking at our doors.

The Holy Bible says Jesus Christ is coming quickly for the
wealthy and poor.

You vow you're a devoted child of God and willing to pay the price.

Will the food you have gathered and stored in your doomsday
bunker truly suffice?

You've been stockpiling for years, getting ready for the day when
there is no more light.

Inside your secret prepper pantry, you've got plenty of
beans and rice.

You think you're prepared for the trial which shall come from
the heist of the world,

You realize the last seal has opened, and the scroll now unfurled.

An angel pours out the vials of wrath and everything goes dark.

The streets and stores are empty. No children playing in the park.

You have faith in the locks of your haven. Things are working
as planned.

You boast, "Guns are my protection," and Satan affirmed,
"You're the man."

The Devil is challenging your faith in God to see if you're obedient
to Yah's commands.

However, unbeknownst to you, this was a test from God. It was
the work of His hand.

As you smile at your fortress, full of strong wine, beans,
rice, and bread,

Watch and pray you doeth not, as the word of Christ Jesus said.

You slumber and sleep under an intoxicating drink nestled
warmly in your bed.

Suddenly, the bunker doors fling open, the security doors
are breeched.

There is an angel standing over your head, and a weary man
kneeling at your feet.

For he's starving for food and water and was told, "here"
he would be fed.

He claims God's voice brought him here. By an angel, he was led.

He tells you all the store shelves are empty, and the springs
of water have run dry.

Hungry and unarmed, he begs and pleads for you to
share your supply.

Your eyes do not see your neighbor with raised hands.

Your ears could not hear your neighbor's cry.

But his request you strongly detest and vowed that he must die.

You closed your eyes and saw the flash from the loaded guns
in both your hands.

You didn't ask him questions, and evil led you to kill this man.

Every day I hear Christians claim they want to be more
like Jesus Christ,

But let the truth be told, you've sold your soul and killed
a man over beans and rice.

Deuteronomy 5:17 (KJV) clearly states, "Thou shalt not kill."[57]

---

57   Deuteronomy 5:17 (KJV).

CHAPTER 11:

God's People Have Problems Too

Adam and Eve, Noah, Abraham, Mary, you, and I. What do all God-fearing individuals have in common? We are all God's people, and we all have had or will have problems. Let's break it down.

God created Adam and Eve. Everything was well in the Garden of Eden until they encountered a problem. Who or what was their problem? The serpent who was also referred to as Satan! Because of this problem (Satan), man fell from God's grace. Adam (man) now had to work or labor for his food. God cursed Eve, the mother of all living, with flesh discomforts that we as women experience today. God gave them another chance, and they went forward, were fruitful and multiplied.

Noah was the builder of the ark and a righteous man of God. He and his family lived during the time when every living being of his generation was full of wickedness and continuous evil. His biggest problem was trying to protect his family from becoming corrupt like the rest of the world. However, because of God's grace, his wife, sons, their wives, and two of every kind of creature on earth survived.

> "But Noah found grace in the eyes of the Lord."[58]
>
> GENESIS 6:8 [NKJV]

> "Then the Lord said to Noah, 'Come into the ark,
> you and all your household, because I have seen that you
> are righteous before Me in this generation.'"[59]
>
> GENESIS 7:1 [NKJV]

Abram, later named Abraham, a new descendent on the new earth through the genealogy of Noah, also had problems. Married for many years, Abram's wife, Sarai, later named Sarah, had not yet born him a child. Wanting desperately to have a child, Abram and Sarai agreed to break God's marriage covenant. Here comes the problem! Sarai (the creator) chose one of her Egyptian maidservants (who had absolutely no say in the matter) to lie with Abram (he agreed) to bring forth his descendants. It became a major problem for Abram when, like Adam, he heeded the voice of his wife, who went against God's will and law. Thus, they broke the covenant of marriage to reproduce. What problem did this cause? Adultery, among other things down the road! But, because of Abraham's faith, we are all a part of his seed.

Next, there's Mary, a young woman who loved God so much that He found favor in her to carry and birth His only begotten Son. Now, you may say, "What problems did Mary have?" Well, first, she

---

58 Genesis 6:8 (NKJV).
59 Genesis 7:1 (NKJV).

had to convince her husband, Joseph, with the help of an angel, she had not slept with another man when he discovered her pregnancy. Second, after giving birth to our Lord and Savior Jesus Christ, raising Him to become and stay a pure young man, and releasing Him to go about God's business, there was the challenge of praying and keeping Him safe. Third and final, she had to be strong when they wrongfully accused Him of no sin, spat on Him, tortured Him, and put Him to death on the tree as she stood there and watched.

The latter individuals are God's people with problems of the past. But what about us or you today? Because of sin, it overwhelms us with problems, especially in these last days. From our nations' leaders right down to the inner core of the earth, God's people have problems. In *Holy Bible: Woman Thou Art Loosed! Edition* (1998), T.D. Jakes writes,

"God's people have problems. We need to face up to that. It's not a matter of lack of faith or of not being saved. It's a fact of life in a fallen world. Problems come with the turf of a world that has been turned upside down by sin"[60] (p. 636).

Your daily stumbling blocks may leave you feeling beaten, bruised, rejected, depressed, or as if you've had a good chastening. Regardless of your circumstances, there is an answer, and His name is Jesus Christ. He is the problem-solver full of faith, hope, and righteousness.

---

60   Jakes, *Holy Bible: Woman Thou Art Loosed! Edition*, 636.

"Now no chastening seems to be joyful for the present, but painful; nevertheless, afterward it yields the peaceable fruit of righteousness to those who have been trained by it."[61]

HEBREWS 12:11 [NKJV]

I need to share my testimony of how my entire family experienced a life-changing event that started with me. But because of our strong faith, we pulled together and got through it with tears of sorrow, joy, and a beautiful blessing.

During my navy career at thirty-five, things took a major turn. While assigned to a seagoing naval vessel, I became pregnant out of wedlock in the year 2001. The displeasure of those appointed over me who received this news only enhanced my stress of having a child. My job position had to be replaced with another sea-ready sailor. I eventually received orders from a shore command to begin my pregnancy transition. Nine months later, I was ready to give birth to my handsome son on my mother's birthday (17 July). He was truly a blessing and gift from God. But there was a problem during the delivery. The umbilical cord became entangled around my son's neck. As he was slowly losing oxygen, the doctor had to perform an emergency cesarean section. These well-trained and experienced doctors, with the help of God, brought us through this serious ordeal. Problem solved, right? Nope! Now for the domino effect.

In August 2002, while on maternity leave and recovering from major surgery, I received a call from my shore commander congratulating me for being selected as a chief petty officer (CPO). Overwhelmed, first with excitement and joy, then anxiety and stress, I realized I had a problem. Let me explain. If you are military or

---

61   Hebrews 12:11 (NKJV).

civilian, you understand that with promotions come problems. What was my problem? In order to be respected and truly welcomed into the unique Senior Enlisted Community, they strongly encouraged me to take part in the grueling CPO initiation or indoctrination.

Did I survive? Yes. Was it painful? Yes! Mentally and physically. Remember, I was a new mom still recovering from a major surgery. However, God is a problem-solver. He allowed good friends, shipmates, and family to be there for me and my son. After completing the reindeer games and receiving orders to report back to a seagoing vessel, there came another major problem. I was told to prepare for a six-month deployment to support Operation Iraqi Freedom and the Persian Gulf War. Topping this off, I had spoken to Daddy frequently, and I could hear in his voice that his health was failing. He had not yet seen his only grandchild. My now five-month-old son and I made it back to Tennessee in time for my daddy to hold his grandson in his frail hands.

On December 2, 2002, God called Daddy to his resting place. My mother was now a widow. Sister, brother, and I were fatherless. My son would never sit at his grandfather's feet. The final nail in the coffin was signing papers giving my mother custody of my son. It was done. No time to grieve. I had to leave my family in order to fulfill my contract and obligation to my country. Each circumstance was a problem. But God made a way. As I continue to grow my faith in God and glean from His wisdom, understanding, and knowledge, with the help of the Holy Spirit, I realize there's an increase in spiritual problems and warfare. It reminds me of moving up the ranks in the military from seaman to CPO. After I was groomed and trained to take on additional authority, responsibility, and accountability, my problem-solving and critical thinking skills also intensified.

Although these temporary storms were difficult and extremely painful, mentally, and physically, the ultimate outcome rewarded me with faith, courage, wisdom, knowledge, and peace to share with others like yourselves who witness what's in my book.

In conclusion, when God's people repeat the phrase "I want to be more like Christ Jesus," understand that we must love and endure those who trespass against us. You may suffer attacks from unbelievers, evildoers, and spirits of the adversary. Therefore, as a child of God, you too will experience problems.

CHAPTER 12:

Using My Pain to Heal Someone Else

I 'd like to start this section with another quote taken from the Woman, Thou Art Loosed! edition of the Bible. If you don't have this Bible, it's alright, just keep reading. If you have this Bible, turn to the book of Romans. On the first page at the very bottom, the writer states that "the best people to help others are not just those who studied life in a book. It is those who lived it out on the stage of reality. You will never be healed until you use your pain to heal someone else."[62]

I was going to teach this topic as a Sunday school lesson at the apostolic storefront church I was attending. My focus point was to discuss, as the title relates, how one person's painful event could help someone else to heal. Little did I know, I was about to experience personal pain from those same individuals I would have been teaching one Sunday morning. Because of my broken marriage induced by "Church Hurt," among other things, I pray that my surrendered pain will help heal someone else.

---

62   Jakes, *Holy Bible: Woman Thou Art Loosed! Edition*, 1241.

If you recall, earlier in this book, I briefly talked about my marriage. Let me remind you. It didn't last long. What were some contributing facts which I believe caused it to fail? First, I asked God for a husband and was not clear why I needed a husband. Second, I was not specific when asking about the man God needed for me. Third, I did not fast, pray, and wait for confirmation from the Holy Spirit with God's approval and blessing. The fire and desire of my flesh only brought me pain and disappointment. In fact, the man I married made it utterly clear. I was not his "good thing," and he was not my Boaz. Inducing the pain, I ignored the "red flags" that were coming to me in my dreams. Yes, I must acknowledge that I prayed and asked God for a husband. We married without being equally yoked and did not wait for God's confirmation and blessing.

Wait, there's more! My pain escalated after receiving a revelation proving the new head of my household and the church family I'd come to love were worshiping a controlling spirit. Last, there's the hurt and pain I felt after explaining to my loving sister, prior to her passing, that continued fellowship and submission under this church's shepherding would further increase our ability to be deceived, controlled, and manipulated. Today, my loving sister sleeps until judgement day, my divorce is final, and there's no more hurt or pain because of God's grace, mercy, protection, and healing power.

"Have mercy on me, O Lord, for I am weak:
O Lord, heal me, for my bones are troubled."[63]

PSALM 6:2 [NKJV]

---

63   Psalm 6:2 (NKJV).

If you have experienced "Church Hurt" and divorce, then you understand firsthand the previously described pain. For some of you, your circumstances may have been much more severe—especially if you held a clergy position within the church and the church board asked you to resign or volunteer to step down. It's like the perfect storm. The loss is devastating. For example, I lost marriage, spiritual leadership, fellowship, place of worship, and trust in those appointed over me. So, how does my pain help heal someone else? Hopefully, hearing my story will allow others to recognize that they are not alone. I need you to get that Jesus Christ died on the tree for our sins. God knows our transgressions and He will heal the brokenhearted and wipe away every tear.

Finally, here are five steps to start your healing today:

1. Find you a quiet place and take a deep breath.

2. Exhale.

3. This step may be difficult, but it's necessary. If you're struggling with pride, let it go. Humble yourself and forgive those individuals who allowed wicked principalities to overtake them and cause your pain.

4. Ask the Holy Spirit (the Helper and Comforter) to coach you through releasing all the pain, grudges, grievances, or resentment you hold against your "Church Hurt" or ex-spouse.

5. Inhale. Exhale. Let it all go, so that you may receive healing.

"Confess your trespasses to one another, and pray
for one another, that you may be healed. The effective,
fervent prayer of a righteous man avails much."[64]

JAMES 5:16 [NKJV]

That being said, I'd like to finish with these questions. Do you believe God will create painful transgressions in your life to test your faith, obedience, self-control, and love for Him? Ask yourself, "Is this pain I'm experiencing today because of my choices or part of God's plan for me? Are the circumstances His will?" If the answer to these questions is "yes," allow His will to be done! Shake the dust from your feet and continue on the journey. Get off the yellow brick road (notice I didn't say gold) and back on the straight and narrow path Yah created for you. Amen and Hallelujah!

---

64   James 5:16 (NKJV).

CHAPTER 13

God Appoints and Anoints Positions in the Church

Today's churches have an abundance of ministries, committees, organizations, and offices in which new members of a congregation can partake. However, to hold one of the highest positions of the church, (i.e., apostle, preacher, priest, imam, rabbi, or other clergy titles) often the individual undergoes hours of divinity education and training. Afterward, he or she undergoes the process of appointment or election to that shepherding position. What happens when someone or a group of individuals within the church skew the criteria for appointment and instead knowingly proclaim a false anointment? Sometimes, when God reveals the truth, the eventual outcome is minor. Other times, the outcome is death. An example would be when internal issues and disputes boil over, and the congregation suffers division. Unfortunately, one of the self-proclaimed leaders departs, taking half the flock with him or her, knowing that their false appointed position and teachings—including love of self—will only enhance the harsh judgment from God. On the other extreme, death can be the outcome not only for the self-appointed and anointed leader, but also for those who did not understand the power of discernment. Historical events vivid in my mind still today are the Jonestown massacre in Guyana and the Waco massacre in Texas. What is my point? If you genuinely believe you've been anointed to shepherd God's sheep and to help build the body of Jesus Christ through His designated offices, it's imperative you know what's in God's Book.

In 1 Corinthians 12:28 (NKJV), the apostle Paul states, "And God has appointed these in the church: first apostles, second prophets, third teachers, after that miracles, then gifts of healings, helps, administrations, varieties of tongues."[65]

I grew up worshipping at the Missionary Baptist Church organization. At an early age, I accepted Christ Jesus, got baptized with water, and received the Holy Ghost. When I became older and intensely studied God's word for myself, it came to my knowledge that my childhood church and many other churches in the local area did not have an appointed apostle or prophet. Although there may have been individuals in the church who could hold these positions, from my recollection, the church never acknowledged them. It was always the head pastor, assistant pastor, deacons, mothers, etc. Now, I used the Baptist Church as an example because my parents raised me Baptist. However, there are millions of churches like this today under different names and denominations, which are missing the first two God-appointed positions. So, if your worship leader denounces God's word and does not believe it's necessary to have an apostle and/or prophet within the organization, and vigorously proclaims he or she is the anointed one, are you being deceived, tricked, and misled?

---

65   1 Corinthians 12:28 (NKJV).

While in the military and afterward, I started attending sanctuaries or services known as non-denominational. I fully enjoyed these times because it was a wonderful feeling of love and worship with people from many backgrounds. Today, I strongly gravitate to the "Five-Fold Ministry," which comprises an apostle, a prophet, an evangelist, a pastor, and a teacher. Because of this structure of teachings, I can humbly say that my hunger for God's wisdom, understanding, knowledge, and increased discernment with the help of the Holy Spirit has magnified my spiritual awareness.

Under the teachings of the "Five-Fold Ministry," I witness church leaders prophesying, laying on of hands, healing, and interpreting tongues from the Holy Spirit. Sadly, I must admit, even today this type of worship does not exist in my childhood church or millions of churches around the world. I glean from these teachings because all the latter Spirit-filled blessings, given by God and Jesus Christ within the Holy Bible, manifest during the worship service. In fact, the twelve appointed and anointed disciples that followed Jesus Christ were also apostles. Each received the gift of prophesying, healing the sick, and raising the dead, among other things. So, I raise the question again: Is it important for you to know whether your spiritual teacher or shepherd was God-appointed and anointed? If you believe it's not important, do you trust that he or she is properly equipping you for the edifying of the body of Christ and for eternal life? Notice how Ephesians 4:11–12 (NKJV) specifically states the requirements of those appointed over you.

"And He Himself gave some to be apostles, some prophets, some evangelists, and some pastors and teachers, for the equipping of the saints for the work of ministry, for the edifying of the body of Christ ..."[66]

Again, notice the biblical protocol God requires. All over the world, there are churches with ten or fewer members, which may include only the pastor, evangelist, rabbi, bishop, etc. On the other side, mega churches are booming with thousands of members. However, evidence has proven repeatedly that the "self-appointed" fall short of being properly equipped (i.e., anointed) to lead the congregation. In each case, it's fair to ask the Holy Spirit, "Is your spiritual leader following God, or are you being deceived by a wolf in sheep's clothing?" God equips apostles; apostles equip prophets. So again, if the latter two are missing or not even welcome in your place of worship, who's equipping your one-man or woman teacher? Just because someone wrote a check, bought the books, sat in a classroom, and got the certificate calling them Dr. Bible Thumper, PhD does not mean they carry the true anointing of God. Allow me to address the elephant in the church. If you're a head teacher of a flock and have vowed to preach the good news of salvation, I pray you hold true to Isaiah 61:1 and reference Luke 4:18.

"The Spirit of the Lord God is upon me; because the Lord hath anointed me to preach good tidings unto the meek; he hath sent me to bind up the brokenhearted, to proclaim liberty to the captives, and the opening of the prison to them that are bound ..."[67]

ISAIAH 61:1 [KJV]

---

66   Ephesians 4:11–12 (NKJV).
67   Isaiah 61:1 (KJV).

Remember, Satan is a well-versed Bible scholar too. In fact, each passing day, there is proof that Satan's leaders and followers are being appointed and equipped to recruit, welcome, and deceive all those who don't ask for the Holy Ghost's help, don't believe in Christ Jesus, and choose not to hear and acknowledge the true word of God.

CHAPTER 14:

Activate Your Blessings Through Fear and Faith

Fear God! Yes, I said, "Fear God!" In order to activate your blessings, one must humble himself/herself before God. Why? Because He is the creator of all things, and like it or not, God has the final judgment on your eternal life. Sure, many wicked and convinced unbelievers, like Satan and his followers, believe they control their eternal destination. However, the only difference between the earthly unbeliever and Satan, God's highest fallen angel, is that Lucifer fears God. For the devil has already experienced the wrath of the Most High and knows his ultimate resting place, the bottomless pit of eternal hell.

> "And do not fear those who kill the body
> but cannot kill the soul. But rather fear Him who is able
> to destroy both soul and body in hell."[68]

MATTHEW 10:28 [NKJV]

---

68   Matthew 10:28 (NKJV).

When you fear the Lord, it cleanses the soul and the body. If you turn back to Psalm 19:9 (NKJV) it states, "The fear of the Lord is clean, enduring forever."[69] Even more so, when we fear God, He provides our daily needs, and we experience an increase in blessings, favors, knowledge, and wisdom.

> "The fear of the Lord is the beginning of wisdom;
> A good understanding have all those who do
> His commandments. His praise endures forever."[70]
>
> PSALM 111:10 [NKJV]

Let God be your fear! Yes, fear Yah (God) and live. Amen.

If I didn't scare you away and you are still with me, because now you understand why it's important to fear God, good! Next, I need you to surrender. Yes, that's it, just surrender. God is waiting for you. Forget about your possessions, what you've done in the past, and what your plans may be for tomorrow. Give your life to God through the Messiah/Yahushua/Jesus Christ, God's only begotten Son. If you really want to experience God's blessings in your life, step out in *Emunah*, Hebrew for faith.

> "Now faith is the substance of things hoped for, the evidence of
> things not seen. For by it the elders obtained a good testimony."[71]
>
> HEBREWS 11:1–2 [NKJV]

Elders mentioned throughout the Holy Bible, such as Enoch, Noah, Abraham, Sarah, Moses, Mary, and Salome (a follower of Jesus

---

69   Psalm 19:9 (NKJV).
70   Psalm 111:10 (NKJV).
71   Hebrews 11:1–2 (NKJV).

who also ministered to Him in Galilee) all had unspeakable faith. Truth be told, if you don't have strong faith, not just some, but strong faith in God, you're not exercising the true potential to tap into your reward of discernment. Each individual received great blessings and favor because they pleased God with their faith.

> "But without faith it is impossible to please Him, for he who comes to God must believe that He is, and that He is a rewarder of those who diligently seek Him."[72]
>
> HEBREWS 11:6 [NKJV]

In today's world, do you believe mankind is diligently seeking God with faith? Or are we caught up in other beliefs, like faith in the universe among other idolatry? One thing is for sure: the year 2020 has tested the faith of every living being here on earth, and our faith will continue to be tested in subsequent years. Once again, you don't have to hear my words. See it for yourself in God's book. The world will continue to experience great sorrow, confusion, corruption, anger, hatred, sickness, and most of all, death. Why? Earth is the devil's hood. He has the authority to indoctrinate those who are lacking and without a strong faith in God. If you are one of many people who stopped having faith in God because of the passing of a loved one, the loss of a business, a job, a home and/or material possessions, allow me to encourage you. Right now, I'm going to ask you to stop, take a moment, and breathe. Close your eyes and recall the faithful elders covered at the beginning of this chapter. Understand, in order to ascend from everlasting damnation to eternal life with the Father, spiritual healing must take place. It's during these times of feeling like we're in the wilderness all alone that God test our faith. He wants

---

72   Hebrews 11:6 (NKJV).

us to add to our faith virtue; we need to be patient, persevere, repent for our sins, and wait for Him.

Allow me to encourage you with this scripture. "And the prayer of faith will save the sick, and the Lord will raise him up. And if he has committed sin, he will be forgiven"[73] (James 5:15 [NKJV]).

Before I close on this chapter, I'd like to give you a prayer assignment. God tells us to ask Him for what we need. So, ask the Holy Spirit (the Helper/Comforter/Messenger) to help you "activate your measure of faith" through Christ Jesus. For "… God has dealt to each one a measure of faith"[74] (Romans 12:3 [NKJV]).

To bring it home, ask it in Christ Jesus' name. That's right. Because here on earth, God gives everyone a measure of faith.

---

73   James 5:15 (NKJV).
74   Romans 12:3 (NKJV).

CHAPTER 15

Hungry for God!

"Oh, taste and see that the Lord is good:
Blessed is the man that trusts in Him!"[75]

PSALM 34:8 [NKJV]

A re you hungry for the Father (God), the Son (Jesus), and the Holy Spirit (Comforter or Helper), whom I will call the "Sous Chef" in this section. Let's head to the kitchen and see what we can whip up to satisfy our spiritual hunger pangs.

On Friday 13, 2020, I woke up and started my morning prayer with my usual ritual. "Good morning Heavenly Father, thank You for Your grace and mercy. Thank You for Your mercy and grace. I thank You for the 'prize of life.' Yes, every day, Father God, You allow me to open my eyes is a 'prize of life.'" As I finished my prayer, my mind immediately shifted to what I was having for breakfast. But I knew I had to spend time with the Lord before dashing to the kitchen to satisfy my hunger pangs. So, I picked up my Bible from the nightstand,

---

75   Psalm 34:8 (NKJV).

and a powerful sensation came over me, which made me realize that the word of God quenches my appetite, feeds my hunger, and is literally food for my soul.

"For He satisfies the longing soul
And fills the hungry soul with goodness."[76]

PSALM 107:9 [NKJV]

As I held my Bible in both my hands, as if I were holding a plate, I started my search to get a better understanding of whether I should "bow" my head or look up to the heavens when I pray. Believe it or not, the Holy Spirit answered this question.

Psalm 5:1–3 (NKJV) says, "Give ear to my words, O Lord, Consider my meditation. Give heed to the voice of my cry, My King, and my God. For to You I will pray. My voice You shall hear in the morning, O Lord; In the morning, I will direct it to You, and I will look up."[77]

After receiving this immediate revelation, I diverted my eyes back down to my hands and how I was holding God's word like a plate. I realized the Sous Chef (Holy Spirit) wanted me to feed on the scriptures referencing being "hungry." Obediently, I flipped to the back of my Bible and searched through the concordance menu for the holy food I needed for this day. Viewing the scriptures listed, I recognized one biblical appetizer served up regularly to every hungry soul with an appetite for God. Then Jesus said, "for I was hungry,

---

76 Psalm 107:9 (NKJV).
77 Psalm 5:1–3 (NKJV).

and you gave Me food, I was thirsty, and you gave Me drink; I was a stranger, and you took Me in"[78] (Matthew 25:35 [NKJV]).

What does all this mean? Allow the Holy Bible to be your plate, hold it in both your hands, and from it feed your mind, body, and soul with the healthy spiritual food that's in it. For, unlike the traditional breakfast of coffee, bacon, eggs, toast, jelly, grits, ham, sausage, biscuits, and rice (non-meat or pork-eaters "judge not" and don't hold this against me), the word of God will neither wear you down nor make you sluggish first thing in the morning before starting your day.

Concluding on a more serious note, I ask again. Are you hungry for God? What is your appetite for Him? If you're still on the fence, let me encourage you to give your life to Jesus Christ. Repent and stay hungry for God starting right now, especially during these fast-approaching times of sorrow and famine. It's a blessing to be hungry and not rude to devour the Holy Book. For it is from the tree of life. John, the author of the last book of the Holy Bible—The Revelation of Jesus Christ—wrote these words concerning those who come out of the great tribulation:

"They shall neither hunger anymore nor thirst anymore ..."[79]

REVELATION 7:16 [NKJV]

Before you are called to your resting place, stay hungry for God. If you have to go through the great tribulation, keep the faith and stay hungry for God. If you truly desire to enter King Jesus' eternal life kingdom, you must stay hungry for God!

---

78   Matthew 25:35 (NKJV).
79   Revelation 7:16 (NKJV).

CHAPTER 16

Look Up! Jesus Is Coming in the Clouds

What would you do if you heard someone shout, "Look! Up in the clouds, it's a bird, no it's a plane, no it's the Great Messiah, Son of God, our Lord and Savior, Jesus Christ?" Would you believe them or continue about your busy way? Well, for me, I would immediately stop what I'm doing and look to the heavens. You ask why? Because God's word clearly tells us Jesus is coming in the clouds, but there's a catch. Understand, no man knows the day or the hour of His return. However, that doesn't mean we should stop looking toward the heavens, day or night, for the miracles, signs, and wonders.

> "In the daytime also He led them with the cloud,
> And all the night with a light of fire."[80]
>
> PSALM 78:14 [NKJV]

---

80   Psalm 78:14 (NKJV).

"Then the sign of the Son of Man will appear in
the heaven, and then all the tribes of the earth will mourn,
and they will see the Son of Man coming on the clouds
of heaven with power and great glory."[81]

MATTHEW 24:30 [NKJV]

Today, man is making ready for every major catastrophic event and doomsday ending. However, are we properly preparing for the return of Jesus Christ? Man has spent millions, even billions, of dollars on bunkers, weapons, non-perishable foods, and even private space shuttles. But will any of this matter? I believe, and I can honestly say with confidence, that none of this will matter. Especially if you haven't repented for your sins, given your life to Jesus Christ, and experienced baptism in water with the Holy Spirit. While we are catapulting to Mars, hunkering down, tunneling under, and power driving ourselves beneath the earth, God's word constantly reminds us to look up and lift our eyes!

"While he was still speaking, behold, a bright cloud overshadowed
them; and suddenly a voice came out of the cloud, saying, 'This is
My beloved Son, in whom I am well pleased. Hear Him!'"[82]

MATTHEW 17:5 [NKJV]

Again, we must give our lives to Jesus Christ while there is time and before God calls us to judgment. Many of us, young and old, believe we will accomplish everything on our "to-do" list or "bucket list." But let's examine the warnings of Jesus' return by the signs that have already occurred and what is happening on the earth.

---

81   Matthew 24:30 (NKJV).
82   Matthew 17:5 (NKJV).

First and foremost, the worldwide COVID-19 pandemic (plague) is still increasing each day. Second, wildfires devastate the West Coast. Third, the East and Gulf coasts are prone to catastrophic roaring waves. Finally, the North is hit by deadly winter blizzards. If you follow global news, other countries around the world are literally being gravely destroyed because of rising waters, earthquakes, volcanoes, and plagues.

> "When these things begin to happen, look up and lift up your heads, because your redemption draws near."[83]
>
> LUKE 21:28 [NKJV]

As I continue to flip through the pages and books of the Holy Bible, I discovered more chapters which account for signs, miracles, and wonders while looking toward the heavens. I found out that Jesus Christ was the only man who descended from and ascended to heaven, as stated in John 3:13 (NKJV). Upon his return to save those of us who believe in Him, there's a verse stating, "… the Lord Jesus is revealed from heaven with His mighty angels …" (see 2 Thessalonians 1:7). Finally, the last book of the Holy Bible, The Revelation of Jesus Christ, makes it truly clear: "Behold, He is coming with clouds, and every eye will see Him, even they who pierced Him. And all the tribes of the earth will mourn because of Him. Even so, Amen"[84] (Revelation 1:7 [NKJV]).

Here's something to think about. Over the last several years, man has noticed and witnessed an increase in extraterrestrial activities in the atmosphere and heavens. Is it possible that what God has hidden from us in the heavenly realm is now being revealed in

---

83   Luke 21:28 (NKJV).
84   Revelation 1:7 (NKJV).

the earthly realm? If there was/is warring in the heavens and if God brings heaven down to earth, is eternity actually invading time? In The Revelation of Jesus Christ, John states, "And when the thousand years are expired, Satan shall be loosed out of his prison. And shall go out to deceive the nations which are in the four quarters of the earth, Gog, and Magog, to gather them together to battle: the number of whom is as the sand of the sea"[85] (Revelation 20:7–8 [KJV]).

If these questions have intrigued you, after reading my book (LOL), I recommend you read Dr. Renny McLean's *Eternity Invading Time*. I'll leave you with a quote from his book:

"The devil's job is to keep you focused on what you can see versus what already exists in the realm of the Spirit. Consequently, you are reduced to believing only what you see."[86]

My last prayer for all humankind is that we take a moment, put away our electrical devices, and look up. Jesus Christ is coming in the clouds!

---

85   Revelation 20:7–8 (KJV).
86   McLean, *Eternity Invading Time*, 6).

CHAPTER 17:

Is Everyday Life
a Prize?

Have you ever just sat in a quiet moment and looked back over your life? In that moment, you realized how many times your assigned angels and the Holy Spirit partitioned God, requesting He not destroy your "life ticket." That's it! That's a wrap! The curtain closed, and the lights turned off for the last time. In the moment, you reflected on how from birth to the present, because of your continued belief and faith in God and Jesus as your Lord and Savior, He delivered you. Yes, every day that you have life, it is a prize. Why is the word "prize" so important? Because God desires us to press forward toward the goal of seeking His treasures and His sublime blessings. He has plans for us. Our lives are precious to Him. We are His beloved.

As a child, I remember accidentally taking my grandmother's (Big Mama's) pills because I thought it was candy. My parents got me to the emergency room to have my stomach pumped before it was too late. Because of Harry Lee and Laura Etta's faith and trust in God, He showed grace and mercy and delivered me. During my young adult years, while serving my country in the navy, I would drink and drive, not knowing how I made it back to the base or the ship. Even more daring, I'd ride as a drunk passenger at night, with a drunk driver speeding over one hundred miles an hour on a two-lane bridge with miles of water underneath in a foreign land. There was no accident. I got back to the ship safely. Recalling this sobering ordeal, I'm not ashamed to honor and trust in God, for He delivered me. Yes, everyday life is a prize.

Stop right now! Take a moment and look back on your life. It was not luck or "the gods" or even the "universe being on your side." God (the Bible says, call him "Yah") delivered you because He loves you and I pray you trust and love Him. When the enemy tries to attack you, and causes you to be afraid, just know it is God and the love of Jesus Christ that will come through and deliver you.

"'But I will deliver you in that day,' says the Lord, 'and you shall not be given into the hand of the men of whom you are afraid. For I will surely deliver you, and you shall not fall by the sword; but your life shall be as a prize to you, because you have put your trust in Me,' says the Lord'."[87]

JEREMIAH 39:17–18 [NKJV]

In the year 2020, the world experienced a major curveball. The scientific, man-made coronavirus (COVID-19) pandemic or plague transformed the life of every human being on earth, including unborn babies nestled comfortably in their mothers' wombs. Today, there is still uncertainty about how this unprecedented plague will affect our future. However, is this a test? Noticed I asked "is" and

---

87   Jeremiah 39:17–18 (NKJV).

not "was." If you have not read the book of Revelation, pick up your Bible, dust it off, and open it to the last written book.

Now, before starting, ask God to deliver you and bless you for reading and receiving His word.

> **"Blessed is he who reads and those who hear the words of this prophecy and keep those things which are written in it; for the time is near."**[88]
>
> REVELATION 1:3 [NKJV]

Again, I ask the question: is the man-made COVID-19 plague a test to bring God's children back to Him, to worship and honor Him and only Him? Again, I say, "Yes." I genuinely believe our all-Mighty God has allowed these circumstances to occur in order to throw humankind a curveball, setting us up for the return of His Son, our King, Jesus Christ.

And for you who are firsthand witnesses; you experience and survived this deadly plague because of absolute faith and love for God. You are now a living testimony in today's time. You persevered. If you came close to death and God said, "Not yet. There's more work for you to do," please understand that you are a living witness that everyday life is a wonderful prize.

> **"Because you have kept My command to persevere, I also will keep you from the hour of trial which shall come upon the whole world, to test those who dwell on the earth."**[89]
>
> REVELATION 3:10 [NKJV]

---

88   Revelation 1:3 (NKJV).
89   Revelation 3:10 (NKJV).

CHAPTER 18

God Wants Eternal Life for You and Me

The bold statement in the above title is based on my personal study of the Holy Bible. There are key words I believe that we as children of God must possess within ourselves that determine whether we experience what Jesus Christ promised us in the New Testament—"eternal life" in the new heaven, on earth with our Father, Abba, Yah, God. It was Jesus' assignment while here on earth to teach and prepare us for eternal life with Him and our Father. From beginning to end, the Bible reference key words, such as fear, faith, believe, love and righteousness, works, and revelation. For me, these key words ascend off the pages of the Bible and demand my full spiritual attention. They are life-changing words that are required and commanded for eternal life with the Father in the New Jerusalem.

Now, I already feel in my spirit some of you are skeptical of the previous statement. That's awesome! Here's where I get to repeat my favorite phrase. Pick up your Bible and dust it off. While demonstrating more of my advanced yeoman skills, I invite you to take part in what I know as fact-finding process and techniques. I've broken down the key words into six sections.

The first and second key words are "fear" and "faith." If you haven't skipped any chapters, you'll remember I previously covered both key words earlier in the book. But, just as a quick refresher, we are to fear God, for He is a jealous God. We must not have any other God before Him. Faith means believing in things not seen but already done. The third key word is "believe." The fourth key words are like a burger and fry combo. I'm combining them because my research shows you can't have one without the other and that's "love and righteousness." The fifth key word is "works," and the sixth key word is "revelation."

Just to lighten the mood, let's go back in time again and dust off that old book called *Merriam-Webster Dictionary* (1828). Now, for the younger generation, way before the computer, the cell phone, and Google, *Webster's Dictionary* (also a book of wisdom and knowledge) was used to find the definition of a word. For example, according to *Merriam-Webster Dictionary*, the transitive verb "believe" means "to consider being true or honest; to accept the word or evidence of" (Merriam-Webster 2022).

Since we are researching how it's used in the Holy Bible, the intransitive verb form of "believe" means "to have a firm or wholehearted religious conviction or persuasion: to regard the existence of God as a fact."

Remember Abram, whose name God changed to Abraham? He was a God-fearing man way past his prime when the Lord told him he would have as many heirs or descendants across the lands as the number of stars in the heavens.

"Then He brought him outside and said, 'Look now toward heaven and count the stars if you are able to number them.' And He said to him, 'So shall your descendants be'."[90]

GENESIS 15:5 [NKJV]

Because Abraham knew firsthand God was real and spoke only truth, he believed in the Lord's word.

"And he believed in the Lord, and He accounted it to him for righteousness."[91]

GENESIS 15:6 [NKJV]

Every day, we get up and believe that our routine is going to be normal. And then, in the blink of an eye, the entire world changed forever. Yes, I said it. The world will never be the same and will never go back to what we considered being normal. Believe me. The year 2020 was a new beginning for individuals seeking to believe in Jesus Christ. Who would have imagined, or better yet, believed that one of many plagues to come would cause people all over the world to get back to the basics of calling on and trusting in the Great I Am and His son Jesus Christ? I believe that out of the thousands or millions of family members that are now sleeping or resting because of COVID-19, many had an encounter with the Holy Spirit prior to taking their last breath, thus giving them an opportunity to say, "Lord, I see You and now I believe. Forgive me of my sins. I know You are real."

---

90   Genesis 15:5 (NKJV).
91   Genesis 15:6 (NKJV).

If you want to be blessed today, regardless of if you believe in Yah's only begotten son, just say, "Lord, I Believe in You."

> **"Jesus said to him, 'Thomas because you have seen Me, you have believed. Blessed are those who have not seen and yet have believed'."[92]**
>
> JOHN 20:29 [NKJV]

Finally, for non-believers that have read this far, first let me say, "Thank you." However, I leave you with this scripture:

> **"You believe there is one God. You do well. Even the demons believe and tremble!"[93]**
>
> JAMES 2:19 [NKJV]

When God created man on earth, His purpose was to grow His family and teach us how to love as He loved. As the population of man grew on the earth, He developed laws instructing us how we should treat one another. In the first books of the Bible, God made it noticeably clear to Moses that we have written and spoken knowledge to love our neighbors as ourselves (see Leviticus 19:18). Therefore, to love our neighbor the way God commands us, we must first love ourselves. However, if you know there's hatred and envy in your heart for your neighbor—be it the brethren in your home, the person next door, or humans around the world—and you're also a self-seeking individual, I encourage you to address this issue immediately by repenting. Otherwise, the probability of you not entering

---

92   John 20:29 (NKJV).
93   James 2:19 (NKJV).

the New Kingdom increases dramatically. Reminder, how you treat your neighbor will show in your book.

"But if you have bitter envy and self-seeking in your hearts, do not boast and lie against the truth. This wisdom does not descend from above, but is earthly, sensual, demonic. For where envy and self-seeking exist, confusion and every evil thing are there."[94]

JAMES 3:14-16 [NKJV]

In addition, He wants us to experience "agape" (derived from the Greek work *agápē*), which means love or "the highest form of love." This Greek terminology agrees with the book of John 3:16, which states,

"For God so loved the world that He gave His only begotten son, that whoever believes in Him should not perish but have everlasting life."

When I read this, it brings me to tears. Why? Because God blessed me with one son. The thought of possibly not being obedient enough to sacrifice my only son for the world we live in today would void every word and belief I previously wrote. Just take a second, right now, and tell God, "Thank You Father!"

Finally, pay attention to His key words. We must believe in Him and love like Him in order to have eternal life. We are not perfect like God or Jesus Christ. However, with the help of the Holy Spirit, we can change before it's too late. Pursue the greatest gift from God. Love!

---

94   James 3:14–16 (NKJV).

When the body of Christ is seeking eternal life with the Lord, why is it important to have righteousness? This time, using modern technology to research righteousness, Google's definition of "righteousness" as a noun is "the quality of being morally right or justifiable." Similar words used are goodness, integrity, honesty, honor, etc. Many of our parents and mentors introduced these words when we were children. These same words as adults, keep us on a straight and narrow path. Organizations like the Armed Forces, Federal or State government, sorority, fraternity, and other special groups all require us to uphold these qualities. If we will maintain righteousness for man, why won't we work harder for our Lord and Savior Jesus Christ? Nevertheless, here are some scriptures to put in your eternal life notebook:

1. "But to you who fear My name, the Son of Righteousness shall arise with healing in His wings"[95] (Malachi 4:2 [NKJV]).

2. "For He made Him who knew no sin to be sin for us that we might become the Righteousness of God in Him"[96] (2 Corinthians 5:21 [NKJV]).

3. "Nevertheless we, according to His promise, look for new heavens and a new earth in which righteousness dwells"[97] (2 Peter 3:13 [NKJV]).

Finally, just like we've pledged at least once in our lives to practice righteousness for mankind, understand the Groom will return for His Bride. Practicing righteousness for the Almighty Father and Son starts now!

---

95   Malachi 4:2 (NKJV).
96   2 Corinthians 5:21 (NKJV).
97   2 Peter 3:13 (NKJV).

> "If you know that He is righteous, you know that everyone who practices righteousness is born of Him."[98]
>
> 1 JOHN 2:29 [NKJV]

> "Little children, let no one deceive you. He who practices righteousness is righteous, just as He is righteous."[99]
>
> 1 JOHN 3:7 [NKJV]

In the beginning, God created the heavens and the earth. His "works" also included making man in Their own image and likeness. The word I want to focus on now is "works." Why is your "works" gravely important to understand? Who should practice how to crucify the "works of the flesh"? And finally, how will "works" affect what's carved in your judgment book and Lamb's book for eternal life? Yes, there are two books and two deaths. Find your Bible, dust it off, and brace yourself for what thus says the Lord. Before we get started, batten down the hatches and secure your spiritual vessel for rough seas ahead!

When we look around today, we see and feel the wonderful works of God. We marvel at the awesome existence of life of every kind, the water we drink and the air that we breathe. Non-believers may argue science or say that the "big bang theory" is how it all got started. My prayer is, by the time you finish reading this chapter, I have made you say, "Hmm," or even better, "I've changed my mind, and I repent."

---

98   1 John 2:29 (NKJV).
99   1 John 3:7 (NKJV).

The word "works" is defined as a "person's (exterior) actions or deeds. In contrast, biblical perspective focuses on inner qualities such as grace or faith."[100] Let's look at an example for both. Your exterior works or deeds may comprise feeding the homeless, cutting your neighbor's lawn, or donating to your favorite charity. The "works of the flesh" consist of adultery, envy, murder, witchcraft, drunkenness and much more, which I'll touch on shortly.

"For the Father loves the Son and shows Him all things that He Himself does; and He will show Him greater works, than these, that you may marvel."[101]

JOHN 5:20 [NKJV]

This scripture is an example of inner or spiritual works. It entails positive things we've already covered, like having faith, love, trust, and belief in God, among other things. If we look back on our lives, we can account for our own personal exterior and inner works, big and small, good, and bad. Why is it gravely important to understand our works from the past, the present, and the future? Because we cannot hide our sins from God. No, not even our thoughts.

As written in the book of Isaiah 66:18 (NKJV), "For I know their works and their thoughts. It shall be that I will gather all nations and tongues; and they shall come and see my glory."[102]

Here is a hard-core fact that many kings, queens, dignitaries, wealthy people, prominent figures, world-renowned individuals, and regular folks like me need to hear and understand. (Those who have

---

100 https://en.wikipedia.org/w/index.php?title=Good_works&oldid=1088177280
101 John 5:20 (NKJV).
102 Isaiah 66:18 (NKJV).

an ear, let them hear what thus says the Lord). Your works under the law of man will not matter or even be justified by God if you do not have faith in Jesus Christ. The very last sentence of Galatians 2:16 states, "… for by the works of the law no flesh shall be justified." Once again, we go back to spiritual works such as faithfulness. So, the second question concerning works asked, "Who should practice how to crucify their "works of the flesh"? Technically, the answer is every man made of flesh. However, Galatians 5:24-25 specifically refers to individuals that are Christ's and who live and also walk in the Spirit." It all boils down to this: your "works" alone can't be justified. You must have faith. Regardless of who you are, without having faith in Jesus Christ—who died for our sins—and refusing to acknowledge Him and accept Him as your Lord and Savior, your lifelong works will not be justified in your judgment book nor the Lamb's book, also known as "the Book of Life."

"For as the body without spirit is dead, so faith without works is dead also."[103]

JAMES 2:26 [NKJV]

Are the hatches of your spiritual vessel still secure for rough waters? Alright, I see a storm up ahead. And if you've ever been in rough water, you'll notice the dark clouds in the distance. Then, the ship rocks forward and aft, or port and starboard. Items that were secured will stay in place, while objects not fastened down will toss to and fro. You may ask, "What does this have to do with 'works'?" Well, pick up your Bible, dust it off, and let's deep dive into the last question.

---

103 James 2:26 (NKJV).

How will "works" affect what's written in your judgment book and God's Book for eternal life? I can see it now. Some of you are scratching your head about this "Book." Every person born, living, and currently resting in peace will have a book with all their external and inner works written in it. From this book, Jesus Christ will present your case (works) as an attorney before the Judge (Yah/God) who sits on a great white throne.

"Then I heard a voice from heaven saying to me,
'Write: "Blessed are the dead who die in the Lord from now on."
'Yes,' says the Spirit, 'that they may rest from their labors,
and their works follow them'."[104]

REVELATION 14:13 [NKJV]

At this age and stage of my life, I consistently thank God for not turning His back on me and not shortening His hand from me, especially while I was out in the world. He gives me the choice and opportunity every day to change my ways, repent, and right my wrongs. I fear Him! Therefore, I humbly steward my daily external and inner works so when I stand before Him to be judged, He will say, "Well done, My good and faithful servant," and my new name will be written in "the Book of Life."

"And I saw the dead, small and great, standing before God,
and books were opened. And another book was opened,
which is the Book of Life. And the dead were judged according to
their works, by the things which were written in the books."[105]

REVELATION 20:12 [NKJV]

---

104 Revelation 14:13 (NKJV).
105 Revelation 20:12 (NKJV).

I can't stress this enough. Let those that have an ear hear what thus says the Lord! These are not my words. I'm only His obedient messenger and yeoman. In fact, this book is a testimony or example of my works. I'm obligated to put before you the words of the Father and Son. Remember, "the Alpha and the Omega, the Beginning and the End," gives us a choice.

So, what happens to individuals whose works are not pleasing to God? What happens when they choose to follow God's Fallen Angel, known as the serpent or Satan? Will God and Jesus Christ omit their names from the Book of Life? If you've been told there is no hell, continue reading:

"And anyone not found written in the Book of Life was cast into the lake of fire."[106]

REVELATION 20:15 [NKJV]

Prayer: "Yah/God, I surrender to you. I repent of my sins. I'll be baptized with water in the name of the Father, Son, and Holy Spirit, so I may have eternal life in the new heaven and new earth." In Christ Jesus' name I pray, Amen and Hallelujah!

By this time, I pray you still have your Bible next to you. If not, go get your Bible and dust it off. Go ahead, I'll wait. Alright, I'd like you to turn to the very back of it. Once there, find a section known as the "concordance." Now, search for the word "Revelation." Notice there are only a few direct scriptures teaching about this word, especially in the Christian Bible. However, if you turn just a few pages toward the front, it will lead you back to the last book of the New

---

106   Revelation 20:15 (NKJV).

Testament, written by John the Apostle, known as *The Revelation of Jesus Christ*. I'll briefly cover this later.

Mats Wahlberg explains in the Stanford Encyclopedia of Philosophy that revelation is "a translation of the Greek word *apokalypsis*, which means the removal of a veil so that something can be seen."[107] The Old and New Testaments describe events that unveil or reveal what's coming before the last days, which will deliver us into eternity with God. So, why is it important to ask the Holy Spirit to give you revelations known to Him? Because based on your measure of faith in Him (Holy Spirit), He will reveal or unveil God's secrets. You will learn how to receive blessings and increase your fortune. The Holy Spirit will prepare you for eternal life with God and His Son.

The Old Testament depended on the laws of kings and the appointed prophets for revelations from God.

> "Where there is no revelation; (a) prophetic vision; the people cast off restraint; But happy is he who keep the law."[108]
>
> PROVERBS 29:18 [NKJV]

God exalted and loved King Solomon, the son of David. Because of God's exaltation, He granted Solomon the desires of his heart. King Solomon received the revelation to lead and provide for the people of Israel.

"On that night God appeared to Solomon, and said to him, 'Ask! What shall I give you?'

---

107 (Wahlberg 2020).
108 Proverbs 29:18 (NKJV).

"Now give me wisdom and knowledge, that I may go out and come in before this people; for who can judge this great people of yours?"

"Wisdom and knowledge are granted to you; and I will give you riches and wealth and honor, such as none of the kings have had who were before you, nor shall any after you have the like."[109]

2 CHRONICLES 1:7,10,12 [NKJV]

In the New Testament, God has granted revelation to man through the revelation of Jesus Christ. For example, as the Apostle Paul took God's word from church to church, he made it clear to the people that the message he delivered was not his own or from the flesh of man:

"But I make it known to you brethren that the gospel that was preached by me is not according to man. For I neither received it from man, nor was I taught it, but it came through the revelation of Jesus Christ."[110]

GALATIANS 1:11–12 [NKJV]

Let us meditate on this scripture for a moment. How many times have you said, "I got a revelation from God!"? I ask that you be extremely careful before unveiling God's mystery shown to you. Verify before you prophesy. Man has often fallen from influential positions and destroyed the lives of those who believed them because of a false revelation being unveiled "not" from or of God through Jesus Christ or from a representative sent by God. Remember the

---

109 2 Chronicles 1:7,10,12 (NKJV).
110 Galatians 1:11–12 (NKJV).

Waco massacre in Texas and the Jonestown massacre in Guyana? For the Father, the Son, and the Holy Spirit cannot lie. Be wise with revelation. Clarify before sharing with others, less you lead them astray.

> "Remove from me the way of lying:
> and grant me thy law graciously." [111]

PSALM 119:29 [NKJV]

Before concluding the power of "revelation," let's return to the final book of the Holy Bible, "The Revelation of Jesus Christ." It's imperative I bring home my point and if you don't remember anything else I've written, I pray you will act on what I'm about to reveal or unveil about this particular "book" in the Holy Bible.

I specifically need to address spiritual leaders of Christianity who have worshipers from all walks of life learning from your teachings. If you vow and claim to be a messenger for God, you have an obligation to ensure God's sheep receive their blessing from "The Revelation of Jesus Christ." If you disagree or oppose this statement, I pray God has mercy on your soul! Now, for those of you who currently worship under any spiritual leaders, and no one in the organization has cracked open the last book "The Revelation of Jesus Christ," it's gravely important you address this matter. What's their delay? If they can't or won't give you a justified answer, run! Finally, if you call or consider yourself to be saved, a child of God, and filled with the Holy Spirit, but you have not read the last book, you are overlooking valuable instructions and your "works" are not done.

---

111 Psalm 119:29 (NKJV).

"The Revelation of Jesus Christ, which God gave Him
to show His servants-things that must shortly take place.
And He sent and signified it by His angel to His servant John,
who bore witness to the word of God, and to the testimony
of Jesus Christ, to all things that he saw." [112]

REVELATION 1:1–2 [NKJV]

"Blessed is he who reads and those who hear the words
of this prophecy and keep those things which are
written in it; for the time is near." [113]

REVELATION 1:3 [NKJV]

After writing the manuscript of this book, I gave my brother Arnett (Smiley) the first opportunity to read my story. I requested he critique everything and give his honest opinion of what he had read. On a blue post-it-note, he presented the following questions. First, he asked, "Have you found inner peace?" Second, "How will readers of your story know if you found peace or you're still working to resolve my issues?" Looking at these two questions and pondering over them quietly and aloud, I realize the importance of closure and clarity. I'm excited to share my thoughts.

The answer to the first question "Have you found inner peace?" is yes, I have found inner peace. By writing this testimony or story and looking back in my mirror, I understood these things are going to be in my book. It is my prayer that the Lord has forgiven my trespasses because I have repented for my sins. I'm at peace because of His grace and mercy. I also found peace by picking up my Bible and

---

112 Revelation 1:1–2 (NKJV).
113 Revelation 1:3 (NKJV).

reading what's in it. I find peace in scriptures about God spiritually healing people after they've experienced molestation, adultery, marriage, and divorce, etc. Whatever I've covered in this book, I know there's a comforting word or a word of correction in scripture. I'm growing in faith, trusting God, and strengthening my righteousness. At this life stage, I can say with confidence, I am at peace, and I will count it all joy.

As for the reader, it's important to me that when you close the last page of this book, you clearly understand why I must serve as a messenger for God the Father, the Son, and the Holy Ghost. I am of flesh, and I'm still filled with sin. We are all filled with sin. No man is perfect. However, that does not mean that I have to act on those things that pull at my flesh. This is the entire purpose of digging deeper into God's word. I ask the Holy Spirit (the Helper and Comforter) to lead, guide, teach, and mentor me along my journey to eternal life in a way that's pleasing to God so that I stay on the straight and narrow path created only for me. No one's journey here on earth is easy, as mentioned in the chapter "God Gives Us a Choice." So, as I get older in life and continue my journey, I know the difference between right and wrong. I'm no longer a child. I understand the consequences of shifting too far left or too far right off the path carved out for me. I will overcome any problem—be it from the past, the present, or the future—because God will fight for me, and I will hold my peace. My purpose in life is to be a faithful messenger and yeoman for Jesus Christ. I acknowledge my strengths and weaknesses as flesh in serving God. I understand the importance of having righteousness and peace in order to walk upright. Peace will also produce joy and righteous living. The joy of the Lord is my strength.

CHAPTER 19

What's in Your Book?

Hey Leper (white) man, what are you mad about? Controlling the world with a silver spoon in your mouth. Hey Israel (brown) man, what are you mad about? That the Leper man blames you for all negative worldly bouts. God, Yah, Abba, Father, what are You mad about? All the broken Commandments and the blasphemy of My Name and abomination of My Holy Word!

To all humankind, honor and acknowledge God the Father, Jesus Christ the Son, and the Holy Spirit the Helper and Comforter before your works here on earth are done and your book is closed, never to open again until judgment day. You still don't believe me? Alright, pick up your Bible one last time. Revelation 20:12 (NKJV) reads, "And I saw the dead, small and great, standing before God, and books were opened. And another book was opened, which is the *Book* of Life. And the dead were judged according to their works, by the things which were written in the books."[114]

---

114 Revelation 20:12 (NKJV).

No matter what you believe, feel, or argue, everyone, the good (worshipers of the one and only true God), bad (worshipers of the ruler and god of darkness), rich, poor, and ugly at heart, will stand before Jesus Christ and the throne of God for Their final judgment. It doesn't matter what color, creed, religion, political party, or sexual orientation you associate with or identify as. Each one of us will have our "own book." In civilian organizations, administrators may use the term Individual Performance Appraisal (IPA). During my time in the navy, my "works" were called a Fitness Report (Fitreps) for the officer and chief petty officers. For the enlisted personnel (E-1 through E-6), their "works" was called an Evaluation (Eval).

In conclusion, I ask again this particularly important question. Do you know what's in your book? Will your name appear in the Heavenly Father's Book of Life or on the list of eternal damnation and destruction? It's your choice. Decide today. Commit yourself to get into a relationship with God. Repent for your sins, choose, believe, and accept Jesus Christ as your Savior. Mark 16:16 (KJV) states, "He that believeth and is baptized shall be saved; but he that believeth not shall be damned."[115] Expedite your need to be baptized with water. This must happen! In fact, if you've joined or became a member of a religious organization and have not yet received the Holy Spirit through baptism, woe to the shepherd and leader who deceived you and led you astray. Even Jesus Christ had to be baptized by John the Baptist! But if you've been baptized with water, get excited about receiving the gift of the Holy Spirit (the Helper and Comforter) who will help you through the journey.

---

115   Mark 16:16 (KJV).

"Then Peter said unto them, 'Repent, and be baptized every one of you in the name of Jesus Christ for the remission of sins, and ye shall receive the gift of the Holy Ghost'." [116]

ACTS 2:38 [KJV]

The saving of a man's soul allows God's angels to rejoice in heaven. Amen and Hallelujah!

---

116 Acts 2:38 (KJV).

ASCEND FROM EVERLASTING DESTRUCTION TO ETERNAL LIFE (WATKINS)

How do you ascend from everlasting destruction to Eternal Life?

How do you walk out of darkness into the light?

How do you change from wrong to right?

Come follow Jesus Christ, for He is the Light!

Are you honing your faith and the works God created for you?

If you're not really sure, here's what you should do

Pick up your Holy Bible and dust it off

Now follow God's instructions from the scriptures taught

From Genesis to Revelation and all the books in between

Your transition will begin for living with the King

Eternal Life with God is what you're working to achieve

And now it's time to roll up your sleeves

Come on! Get to work. You must sow the good seeds.

For when your final book is opened, the King will be pleased

When the ascend from everlasting destruction to Eternal Life is complete,

God will say, "Come stand on my right-hand side, for you are now one of My sheep

You followed My instructions, love, faith, and good works I see

Your new name is in the Book of Life!" As you give praises to the King

Sing "Holy, holy, holy!" As you, sit at the Savior's feet.

Written by Laura Elizabeth Watkins

MY MORNING PRAYER (WATKINS)

Holy Spirit, I thank Yah, the Father for this day

He gave me the roof over my head.

I thank Him for the bed from which I rise

I thank Him for the floor beneath my knees

The air I breathe is thanks to Him.

I thank Him for love, grace, mercy, and peace

He gave me the prize of life.

Holy Spirit, I ask the Father to pour into me wisdom, understanding, and knowledge

I ask the Father for an increase in discernment

Thank the Holy Spirit for being my comforter.

I give God all the honor and praise. He is the Alpha and Omega, the Beginning and End.

He is the one and only true God

Holy Spirit, I ask You to continue helping me transition and ascend from everlasting destruction to eternal life.

I ask these things in Christ Jesus' name, Amen, and Hallelujah!

Written by Laura Elizabeth Watkins

MY FINAL PRAYER REQUEST

Concerning the heavenly angels of God, I pray that one sinner here on earth will repent, be baptized with water, saved by reading this book, and pick up the Holy Bible and dust it off to bring more joy to heaven. (ref. Luke 15:7,10 NKJV)

Bibliography

AV1611.com. 2022. *"KJV Dictionary."* Accessed May 29, 2022.
https://av1611.com/kjbp/kjv-dictionary/fast.html

McLean, Renny. 2005. *Eternity Invading Time*. Altamonte: Advantage Books.

Merriam-Webster, s.v. "believe (v.)," accessed May 26, 2022,
https://www.merriam-webster.com/dictionary/believe

Merriam-Webster, s.v. "abomination (n.)," accessed May 29, 2022,
https://www.merriam-webster.com/thesaurus/abomination

Jakes, T.D. 1998. *Holy Bible, Woman Thou Art Loosed! Edition*.
Nashville, Thomas Nelson.

Oxford University Press, s.v. "accompany (v.)," accessed May 26, 2022,
https://www.lexico.com/en/definition/accompany

Oxford University Press, s.v. "adultery (n.)," accessed May 26, 2022,
https://www.lexico.com/en/definition/adultery

Raising Children Network. 2020. "Child development: the first five years."
Accessed August 10, 2021, https://raisingchildren.net.au/newborns/
development/understanding-development/development-first-five-years

Smith, Jerod. 2021. "Identity and Purpose Summit." Interview by Faith Wokoma.
June 2021. Video, 30 minutes, https://askdoctorfaith.com/product/identity-
and-purpose-summit/

Wahlberg, Mats. 2020. "Divine Revelation." *Stanford Encyclopedia of Philosophy*.
Last modified July 17, 2020. https://plato.stanford.edu/entries/divine-revelation/

Watkins, Laura. 2021. *"Ascend from Everlasting Destruction to Eternal Life."*
What's in My Book, Ascending from Everlasting Destruction to Eternal Life,
BookBaby, 2022.

Watkins, Laura. 2021. *"My Morning Prayer."* Nashville, April 10.

Index

A

Abraham 30, 45, 46, 47, 48, 49, 55, 56, 72, 88, 89
Activate 71
Appoints 65

B

baptized 39, 48, 66, 97, 104, 105, 108
Bible 4, 39, 43, 52, 57, 75, 76, 77, 84, 85, 87, 90, 93, 95, 97, 101, 103, 106, 108
Blessings 71
books 13, 68, 81, 90, 93, 96, 103, 106

C

chasten 39
Choice 49, 102
Clouds 79

D

deceive 15, 69, 82, 93
destruction viii, 7, 11, 17, 27, 34, 35, 48, 52, 104, 106, 108
Dust 1, 23

E

Ear 29
Eternal x, 87, 106
Everlasting x, 106

F

Faith 32, 71, 88
Fasting 23, 25
Follow 39, 40

G

Gives 49, 102
glory 5, 7, 51, 80, 94
guide iii, 1, 17, 33, 34, 35, 37, 39, 102

H

Heal 61
Helper 11, 63, 74, 75, 102, 103, 104
Hungry 25, 53, 75

I

increase 4, 36, 59, 62, 72, 81, 98, 107
inspired viii
instructions 20, 30, 36, 39, 50, 100, 106, 107

J

joy 42, 58, 102, 108
judged 14, 43, 96, 103
Junk 7

K

kill 54, 71
kisses x, 51

L

Listen 17, 29
Look 46, 79, 89
love iii, v, vii, 3, 4, 21, 29, 34, 41, 49, 51, 60, 62, 64, 65, 67, 84, 85, 87, 88, 90, 91, 94, 107

M

mental 11, 12, 19, 20
Mind 19
Mirror 3

N

narrow 64, 92, 102
nations 57, 82, 94
night 79, 84, 98

O

obedient viii, 42, 43, 50, 53, 91, 97
O Lord 35, 62, 76
Overwhelmed 58

P

prayer viii, 2, 8, 9, 12, 19, 24, 25, 27, 34,
    64, 74, 75, 82, 93, 101
prize 75, 83, 84, 85, 107
Problems 55, 57

Q

queer 12
questions 3, 12, 19, 23, 51, 54, 64, 82,
    101
quickly 10, 36, 52

R

Renewal 19
reveal 3, 98, 100
reward 19, 43, 73

S

Savior 35, 39, 57, 79, 83, 92, 95, 104, 107
soul ix, 8, 11, 25, 34, 54, 71, 72, 76, 77,
    100, 105
spiritual i, vii, ix, 3, 4, 8, 9, 13, 15, 16, 19,
    29, 30, 31, 36, 37, 39, 59, 63, 67,
    68, 73, 75, 77, 87, 93, 94, 95, 100

T

taste 75
technology 19, 29, 36, 92
tremble 29, 90

U

unbeliever 71
understanding vii, x, 2, 8, 10, 17, 19, 26,
    30, 59, 67, 72, 76, 107
universe 73, 84

V

value 5
vessel 13, 50, 58, 59, 93, 95
voice 32, 49, 53, 56, 59, 76, 80, 96

W

wisdom vii, x, 2, 9, 17, 19, 30, 51, 59, 67,
    72, 88, 91, 99, 107
woman 5, 16, 56, 68
works v, ix, 8, 43, 87, 88, 93, 94, 95, 96,
    97, 100, 103, 104, 106, 107

Y

Yah v, 49, 51, 53, 64, 72, 84, 87, 90, 96,
    97, 103, 107
yeoman 21, 50, 87, 97, 102
yoked 62